KU-145-309

THE
ICE KITCHEN

For my Ben.

Is the freezer door shut?

SHIVI RAMOUTAR

THE
ICE KITCHEN

Fast Fresh Food to Fill Your Family and Your Freezer

HarperCollins*Publishers*

Contents

Why you need this book

We are all time-strapped, wallet-wary, environmentally aware and mindful of what we consume, while still wanting to enjoy exciting, flavoursome homemade meals at the drop of a hat. Basically we want it all. And you know what? We can have it all!

Freezers (and their contents) have long been deemed unfashionable and retro, bringing to mind highly processed, ice-burned or long-forgotten meals (who knows exactly what *that* was?) that inevitably get thrown out after being discovered in the frozen-pea-scattered, over-iced depths a few years down the line.

Let me introduce you to *The Ice Kitchen* Method of cooking, eating and (if it isn't too over the top to say) of living! All the hard work and planning has been done for you: you will rarely need scales to measure out ingredients; there will be no waste; there is always a use for that random carrot/chicken breast/lemon half; you'll be able to tailor meals to your fussy child/partner/guest; and dishes will be packed with vegetables, goodness and flavour. You'll learn to cook once and eat twice; avoid expensive, often insipid, and likely nutritionally poor takeaways and instead indulge in simply delicious meals that are wholesome, homemade, cost-effective and quick, and where you know exactly what has gone into your food. All this is possible within that icy realm of the kitchen that we all already have . . . the freezer!

According to an Open Access Government article with research carried out by Gousto, £494 million worth of food is thrown out every week in the UK (about eight meals a week per household, says WRAP), with vegetables topping the list. Over a third of us forget what we have bought in our weekly shop and usually cook too much food. A fifth of us throw out food because we don't plan our meals properly. Freezers are the perfect tool for reducing this monumental food waste and making it easier to meal plan. According to WRAP, using frozen food can **reduce household food waste** by as much as 47 per cent.

Freezers are also the way forward for **making your shopping cost-effective**, as you can buy produce in bulk (which tends to be cheaper than buying smaller-packaged quantities) and cook larger batches of meals to freeze for future use, thus making the cost per person per meal cheaper overall.

Freezers **make the most of seasonal produce**, which again tends to be cheaper when bought at the right time of year. When you can bulk-buy and freeze food, either by cooking into a meal, or by freezing individual ingredients when they are fresh (vegetables and berries, for example), you'll end up in the advantageous position of being able to extend food's seasonality, enjoying it for many more months without the air miles of imported produce!

Freezing food **locks in its nutritional value**. Using the freezer to store ingredients and meals literally presses 'pause' on fresh food; taking something out of the freezer presses 'play', meaning that you can enjoy that ingredient or meal at a time convenient to you, with the same level of nutritional value as the day that you froze it! In some form or another, most of us already have this perfect preservation tool already taking up space in our kitchen.

Given our busy, **time-strapped lifestyles** it makes so much sense to utilise this clever tool to ensure you get delicious, fulfilling and wholesome meals, without the effort: **make a meal once and eat from it at least twice**! What's not to love about having a range of delicious, tailored-to-your-tastes meals for the whole family (whatever this means to you) right at your fingertips, whether during the mad midweek rush, or the relaxed feasting of the weekend?

Given that most of us have a freezer, it really surprises me that so few of us really know how to make the most of it, how to use it properly, or just feel comfortable enough with the freezing and defrosting process. Food from the freezer doesn't have to mean fish fingers, cardboard-textured pizza and potato waffles. Yes, it's great for storing leftover bolognese and other comforting feasts, but it can also be a clever tool to give you so much more. Nearly every meal in *The Ice Kitchen* can be cooked straight from frozen so no need to plan ahead.

The Ice Kitchen Method is all about putting this right! You will find chapters filled with deliciously simple breakfast and brunch ideas (from humble sweet oats to decadent savouries); exciting meals and flavoursome snacks that go from freezer to table, perfect for weekend feasting and midweek eating; complete ready-made meals for those days that you only have time to open and close your freezer and oven door; puds and iced treats that you won't want to live without; and hacks, solve-all sauces and bases that can transform into a rainbow of quick meals, making life (and preparing a gorgeous homemade meal) that little bit easier. Let's face it, we ALL deserve that. Think warming, freezer-to-table earthy one-pots, decadent puds, cool desserts, fresh (yes!) brunches and, my personal favourite, the Salvation section: pure 'saucery' via ready-to-go sauces (some bagged and some frozen into ice-cube portions) along with clever bases that you *need* to have stashed in your freezer. These can be transformed into a host of dishes, with ingredients of your choice for quick-fix midweek magic meals. And my Salvation Suppers: Feasts-in-Foil are exactly that: complete 'ready meals' that you can put together and enjoy with all the ease of shop-bought ready meals but without the unnecessary additives and excess salt, sugar or fat.

The Ice Kitchen

Harking from a Caribbean background of writing tropical carnival-coloured recipes choc-a-block with flavour, it should come as no surprise that this book contains recipes that are packed with some subtle (and not so subtle) inspiration from across the globe.

At the same time, it also celebrates those lovely homely recipes that also have an important place in my life – like a quick pot pie, eaten on the sofa under a blanket when the dreaded sniffles rear their head, or, for those that know me and my obsession with ice cream, my ultimate ice cream sandwich (for any occasion!).

Having recently welcomed a second (very hungry!) son into my family, now more than ever I find I need swift, but nonetheless happy-making food that is packed with goodness, flavour, convenience and comfort – in every sense of that word. *The Ice Kitchen* wholly represents the way I cook and eat, from midweek meals to weekend feasts for my family, friends or sometimes just for me (in those rare moments that I catch myself alone at mealtimes!). I do also try to do my bit for the environment, making the best efforts to avoid wasting food, eating seasonally, (where possible) and using up whatever we have in the kitchen first, before resorting to buying more ingredients (often referred to as a fridge forage – what a superb term!). It's also a fantastically cost-effective way to eat!

In the light of the above, I like to make food that can easily be switched up to take into account what ingredients I *do* have immediately available; food that can be tailored for children and fussy eaters (young and old alike, I may add); and more importantly, food that is full of flavour. The recipes are to inspire your own versions of freezer meals, so feel free to twist recipes, change ingredients and experiment with flavours. And when I say freezer meals, dispel that image of grey pre-packaged meals; I am talking about a rainbow-coloured, flavour-riddled array of breakfasts and brunches, meals that go beyond lasagnes and bolognese, sharing snacks, clever midweek freezer hacks, puds and cold desserts for you to paw over. Delicious food that just happens to be perfect for the freezer, and thus perfect for simple but satisfying dining.

There are handy guidelines in many of the recipes to help you make the dishes entirely your own, so you can use up those last few sad-looking vegetables lurking in your fridge, swap the pork mince for that beef that needs using up, or simply change the vibe of a dish from a traditional British flavour to a sun-drenched tropical one with the addition of a few spices.

I hope this book lets you realise the amazing capabilities of your freezer. and how it can transform your weekday

meals, weekend feasts and everything in between. By simply learning a few tricks and tips and understanding how truly easy it is to use this resource (one that pretty much all of us already have in our homes), you will make your life easier and mealtimes more efficient, without any compromise on flavour. Hand on heart (and this may sound over dramatic!), I don't actually think I could live without mine now.

A note on kids and fussy-eaters
All recipes can be tailored to accommodate any fussy eater. Essentially in my home we all eat the same meal – not only does it make mealtimes simpler, but it encourages fewer fussy eaters too. However, I portion off the kids' servings before I add seasoning or strong flavours such as chilli, then keep a separate section in my freezer for the kids.

Whilst I think it best for kids to learn to love veg for veg's sake, there are times when you need to squeeze in as much goodness as possible with minimal pain. A last resort is to 'sneak' extra vegetables into meals. Add a handful of rough-chopped courgette, carrot, spinach and aubergine to Swift Salvation Tomato Sauce (see page 115), simmer until softened then blitz until smooth. Having this frozen in portions to use as a pasta or pizza sauce is a great way to inject extra veg. Main dishes with rich flavours such as Peanut Stew (see page 57), or Beef & Prune Tagine (see page 76) are perfect vehicles to hide veg (I love choc-a-blocking the former with leafy greens).

The best way to freeze their versions of our meals is in ice-cube trays, or even specially purposed silicone trays (so easy to find online or in supermarkets). The smaller portions mean I can defrost exactly the amount of cubes I think my kids will eat for a particular mealtime, which, if you have children you will know can vary wildly across the day. This cuts down on waste (much to the dog's disappointment, I may add!) but tiny portions will defrost a lot more quickly too. Once the meals are frozen solid in the trays, I pop them out and store in resealable freezer bags, clearly labelled with the name and date frozen, and 'file' them in the kids' section in my freezer.

I tend to defrost meals for the kids in the fridge, either popping the cubes out the night before or first thing in the morning. Any final defrosting can be dealt with by the defrost setting on the microwave; simply cover the plate of food and microwave in 30-second bursts until the food is fully defrosted, breaking up and mixing after every burst to ensure more even defrosting. If I'm warming a sauce, stew or casserole I would keep it covered and heat in the microwave on high, again in 30-second bursts with some stirring in between, until piping hot. This is slightly different to how I deal with large portions of meals, which I tend to not defrost in the microwave (see page 14) but given the more urgent time pressure when dealing with kids (read: meltdown/tantrum avoidance) I am happy to prioritise speed over perfect texture!

How to freeze

1
Food must be cool before being put into the freezer

Putting warm food into the freezer will increase the temperature of the freezer and can cause food that's already in there to start defrosting. To cool something down quickly, create an ice bath by putting the hot food into a bowl and putting this bowl into a larger bowl filled with ice and cold water.

2
Storage must be airtight

This prevents freezer burn and keeps moisture in to avoid dried-out food. There are a host of different storage products you can use out there, but reusable, resealable bags (you can find excellent silicone versions now too) are conveniently available and great for making the most of small spaces. The fact that you can wash and reuse them is brilliant too. If you choose to do this, try to keep bags for raw food separate from bags for cooked food. When you wash them, just double-check that there are no holes in the bag. A brand of this type of reusable, resealable freezer-friendly silicone bag that I have fallen head over heels for is Stashers. They can be placed directly into the oven or into a pan of hot water, so the freezer to table way of *The Ice Kitchen* Method really becomes just that. So clever! **When using bags, always ensure you remove excess air,** not only to prevent freezer burn, but also to make better use of the space in small freezers. You can go all out and use a straw to suck out any excess air on a partially sealed bag before totally sealing, but using your fingers to squeeze out any excess air before sealing is usually sufficient.

Foil is great for certain foods too, like chicken drumsticks, or random odds and ends. Given the war on single-use plastics (and I am currently making it my mission to reduce our use of plastic at home), I am trying to reduce my reliance on cling film – the best alternative is the aforementioned silicone bags. I tend to stick to my reusable, resealable, airtight silicone Stashers. If I freeze baked goods, I tend to foil-wrap then pop into a silicone bag.

If you need to use a container (for ice cream, granita, etc.), make sure it is freezer-friendly. I tend to use good old Tupperware, with a proper lid. Where possible, use containers that are the right size, so don't put a small amount of ice cream in a massive Tupperware (not only is this a waste of freezer space but it can also cause freezer burn).

3
—

Freeze flat where possible

Pop the meal into a resealable bag and remove any excess air before sealing (see opposite). Then it's as simple as spreading the food out as flat as possible when the sealed bag is laid flat. The additional benefit is that food freezes more quickly, thereby stopping large ice crystals from forming and thus helping to maintain the quality of the food.

4
—

It is ALL about freezer filing

The key to optimising your freezer (and actually eating the food that's in there as opposed to binning random bags months later) is the way you store and label your *Ice Kitchen* food! Write clearly what the meal is, the date you are freezing it and any freezer to table guidelines for defrosting and reheating: either 'hob' or 'oven', along with temperature and time (all clearly set out in the recipes). This means that when *hanger* strikes, you can flick through your freezer 'file' (see right) and make a choice depending on how much time the meal will take to be ready. Most freezer storage bags have a white area to make it easy for you to mark down the details with your Sharpie (or other permanent pen), but as I try to wash and reuse freezer bags where possible, I use freezer tape to write on and stick to the container or bag (don't do what I've done in the past and use my son's washable marker pens). And

permanent pens work well on foil too. If you have a mix of raw and cooked foods in the freezer, think about **using coloured pens** to easily identify which is which – or use the clever silicone resealable bags that are colour-coded!

Once frozen flat, I **create a filing system**. I put the most recently frozen food at the back of each section to ensure I'm getting through the **oldest frozen food first** – 'first in, first out' is a good way to remember it! I haven't got the largest freezer so I have to be quite clever with the usage of space; once my meals are frozen flat I then 'file' them upright. If freezing anything wrapped in foil (the Eastern Stuffed Peppers on page 50, for example), I find it useful to mark which way is up so it goes into the oven the correct way up when you reheat it.

I then create separate rows for each shelf/area: one with the quick bases such as you'll find in the Salvation Suppers chapter; one for whole meals from the Main Meals chapter, like Peanut Stew, Creole Gumbo and Beef Rendang (see pages 57, 40 and 77); and another for things from the Snacks and Sharers chapter, like Thai Crab Cakes and Korean Cauliflower Poppers (see pages 144 and 148). I tell you, there is nothing more satisfying than flicking through ordered files of food – other than eating it, of course!

5
—
Clever portioning/serving sizes

Now this is really the key to *The Ice Kitchen* Method. Let's face it, if you're already in the kitchen you might as well add on a few extra minutes to your prep time to double, or even triple the recipe. You're going to be going through the process anyway so chopping a few extra veg here and there makes TOTAL sense, rather than having to start completely from scratch another time. **Two (or even three!) meals for the 'price' of one** is how I look at it. With this in mind, although I usually write recipes to serve 4 (adult portions, so you'd probably get extra portions if feeding kids), I've doubled the quantities in this book, so most of the recipes serve 8 – 4 'For Now' and 4 'For Later'. It really is a case of cook once, eat twice – unless you are feeding a crowd, in which case I'd actually suggest scaling up again so that you can make something to serve 10–12 and still have a meal for two for another day!

Portioning up meals is also a great way to ensure that you don't have food wastage by having to defrost a larger amount and eat only a little of it. I tend to freeze my meals in portions of two; occasionally I will freeze a few meals in individual servings for those last-minute moments when dining solo. Bread is great to have sliced and ready to go with a little greaseproof paper separating each slice to avoid any sticking. Ice-cube trays are gold dust for portioning sauces, butters and dressings, as well as storing leftover ingredients like wine, citrus juices and stocks. Sometimes there is a need for something in between ice-cube size and Tupperware; in these situations I always have freezer-friendly snack boxes or dressing pots handy.

When freezing dressings, sauces and other things in ice-cube trays, I always pop them out of the trays once frozen and then store in labelled freezer bags to save space.

6
—
Have a freezer jam-packed with food

A full freezer requires less energy to run and is therefore more cost-effective. But be wary of filling it with lots of unfrozen produce at one time as this may bring down the temperature inside the freezer.

7
—
Frozen meals should be eaten within 3–6 months

While frozen food can be kept indefinitely, over time taste and texture will be altered, so my general rule of thumb is that **most frozen meals should be eaten within 3–6 months**. So do make sure you date things clearly to ensure you eat any food that is about to hit this deadline first.

8
—

Freeze food as fresh as possible

This is to make sure you capture it at its best – not only quality-wise but nutritionally too. Although freezing often doesn't affect the flavour of ingredients (actually, some cooked dishes come out of the freezer tasting better than freshly cooked – think stews, soups, casseroles, curries), it can often affect texture, so you have to be clever as to how you use certain frozen items, like berries, which tend to become soggy once defrosted (but are perfect for using in compotes, smoothies, cooked puds and ice cream). And remember, **you can refreeze previously frozen raw ingredients as long as they have changed state** and have now been cooked.

9
—

Your freezer needs to be regularly defrosted

To be energy efficient, your freezer needs to be regularly defrosted to get rid of ice build-up (ice not only takes up space where you can store your food, but also uses up more electricity as the freezer needs to work harder to keep cold). Frozen food will be fine for a few hours in the fridge if all packed together.

10
—

Don't forget freezer 'safety'

It may sound very basic, but make sure the freezer door is properly closed, and open it only when necessary. If the freezer door hasn't been firmly closed and food has already begun defrosting, it cannot be refrozen and must be put into the fridge to be eaten as soon as possible.

How to defrost

Defrosting food safely is so important and a lot of us are quite nervous about it, so we often end up microwave-nuking wonderful meals and spoiling the texture and taste. There are some foods that cannot be cooked straight from frozen – large bone-in joints of meat will need to be thoroughly defrosted before being cooked and it's usually always advisable to defrost raw poultry fully before cooking, unless otherwise stated.

Cooking straight from frozen

While it is usually best to defrost in the fridge first, most of the dishes in *The Ice Kitchen* have been created so they can be cooked straight from frozen.

As you may not always be cooking the full amount of a recipe from frozen, if you've frozen in smaller portions, for example, the freezer to table times noted throughout the book may need to be reduced accordingly, so don't forget to check in now and again to see how it's getting on.

Foods can be cooked straight from frozen in the oven, on the hob or in the microwave. Some types of silicone bags, such as Stashers, can be placed directly from the freezer into the oven, a pan of hot water, or the microwave.

• **HOB** – When using the hob to defrost food or to reheat defrosted food, I'd suggest adding a splash or two of water to the pan to prevent the food from catching. It needs to be stirred quite often and the lid should be kept on when not stirring to prevent the food from drying out. When using the hob for freezer to table dishes, the key point here is cooking at a low temperature first to thaw out the food, gently breaking it up as you go along, then increasing the temperature so that the meal is piping hot.

• **MICROWAVE** – You have to be wary with what foods you choose to defrost or cook from frozen in the microwave as the texture can be affected; you can end up with hot patches of food alongside frozen patches. Whether you are defrosting or cooking from frozen, I would advise microwaving in short bursts of 20–30 seconds and checking and stirring after each burst. Wherever the microwave is a suitable place to defrost or cook one of my recipes without affecting its texture and taste, I have included notes alongside the recipe.

- **OVEN** – When using the oven, once again you have to ensure that the food is piping hot throughout. As the oven time for cooking from frozen is longer than cooking from defrosted, there is greater chance of the food drying out, so cover with a lid or foil, where necessary, for the majority of the cooking time; you can then cook uncovered for a smaller amount of time to crisp up the dish. Given the variation in baking trays, dishes and also the amount of frozen food you may be cooking, you do need to check in near the end of the cooking time, as there may be naturally slight variations in timings here and there.

Defrosting before cooking

For any dishes that need to be defrosted before cooking, here are some basic guidelines:

- Ideally leave it in the fridge for a slow thaw. This is the safest way to defrost food (at a temperature that doesn't allow quick growth of harmful bacteria) while preserving its texture and taste. Leave food in the packaging that it was frozen in and put into a shallow bowl (in case any water is released during the thaw) and into the fridge. With most meals and large joints of meat this will usually require an overnight fridge thaw, sometimes a day or two in the fridge for larger items; smaller meals can often be put into the fridge early morning for a meal that evening. Smaller items, like those in the Snacks and Sharers chapter, may need less time to defrost, maybe even just a few hours in the fridge,

depending on size. Uncooked pastry takes just a couple of hours to defrost at room temperature (yup, you can leave this one out on your counter).

- For quick defrosting, you can place food in a tightly sealed bag (so no water leaks in) and put into a bowl of iced water, topping up with ice, or changing it every 30 minutes, to ensure that it stays cold (defrosting in warm water, or even at room temperature, increases the chances of harmful bacteria contaminating the food). You can also defrost quickly in the microwave, but I tend to avoid using this method as it can be quite an inconsistent way to defrost and there is greater chance of pockets of the food being cooked while others remain frozen, meaning that the quality and texture of the food once cooked can be greatly compromised. You can also find quick defrosting trays now that speed up defrosting time by almost ten times.

- Generally speaking, I very rarely leave food out at room temperature to defrost as this method of defrosting can increase the risk of harmful bacteria contaminating the food.

- Halve the 'from frozen' cooking guidelines if defrosting first.

How to use this book

In addition to the cooking method, freeze and freezer to table information given with each recipe, you'll also notice the following helpful symbols by each recipe, which tell you at a glance what you need to know:

vegetarian

Does what it says on the tin

quick prep

15 minutes or less of preparation

one-pot

Recipes that only require one receptacle for cooking

chop 'n' change

Recipes that can be changed to take into account what you have in your kitchen, or what flavour profile you fancy, or even portioned up and flavoured differently.

TRY ADDING:
Suggestions of ingredients you can add to jazz up the dish, give it a twist, up the veg quantity, or help use up a glut!

SWAP:
Ideas of ingredients that would work as well as the original suggested recipe, in case you fancy a different twist.

➜ *Try with*
The accompaniments, sides and extras I would devour the dish with. Feel free to experiment and try out your own additions.

At the back of the book, I've thrown in some further appendices. The first appendix is a 'What to Do With' section that provides helpful tips to preserve leftovers and what to do with any food gluts. The second groups together all the vegetarian and vegan recipes (or suggesting ways that ingredients can easily be swapped to make them vegetarian or vegan). The third groups together recipes that use similar ingredients so that you can batch-cook a few recipes together, saving time and effort and avoiding food wastage. The fourth appendix suggests make-ahead menus for feasting.

A note on ingredient measurements/quantities

I have tried to make the ingredient quantities (using tablespoons and teaspoons) as accessible as possible so you have the minimal need for scales. I've also used grams for liquid measurements (it's easier to weigh up liquids when you already have the scales out, than bending down to read the bottom of a meniscus [measuring really does bring out the GCSE chemist in me!]).

I have tried to list measurements of ingredients that should be easy to find in a supermarket, like 1 x 400g tin of X, or sausages in packs of six. However, when you can't find the exact measurement or weight of an ingredient, for example sweetcorn can be found in 198g tin or a 195g tin, it doesn't matter so much. The idea is that the recipes can be tailored a bit to take into account what you do have available, or what you can find. Of course, be sensible about this, I wouldn't throw in 500g of sweetcorn when the recipe asks for a 195g tin, but 200g to 300g may be fine. The only time this rule can't apply is when you are baking; you have to be a little more precise with these measurements, unless otherwise stated I'm afraid!

Unless stated otherwise:

- All eggs are medium.
- Butter is unsalted.
- Oil can be olive, vegetable or rapeseed.
- Teaspoons and tablespoons are level.
- The oven should always be pre-heated.
- Unless specified, onions can be red or white.
- I use sea salt flakes. In the handful of recipes where I ask for a specific quantity of salt, this will be with regard to flakes rather than cooking salt or table salt, where you will need to reduce the amount that you add to recipes.

Breakfast & Brunch

It was so tricky to bundle these recipes into just one chapter, because, let's be honest, sometimes we want morning muffins in the afternoon and the Sweet Potato & Chorizo Hash definitely works at dinnertime. Whenever you choose to eat these meals, they provide a great start, middle and end to your day, all from your freezer. Bish bash bosh.

Zap-N-Go Morning Muffins

MAKES 12 MUFFINS (4 FOR NOW, 8 FOR LATER) | 10 MINUTES PREP | 20 MINUTES COOKING

Muffins have always struck me as a bit of a 'pretend' morning food, kind of like cake fancy-dressing as breakfast. But these easy-to-make muffins not only tick the 'tastes like cake' box, but are also actually packed full of virtuous ingredients. A few seconds in the microwave and you can be running out of the house with a warm meal packed with just what you need to start your day (or continue it, or end it ...).

7 tbsp butter (about 100g), melted and cooled

2 eggs

5 tbsp yoghurt (natural, ideally)

6–9 tbsp runny honey, depending on how sweet you like it

1 tsp vanilla extract

200g wholemeal (or plain) flour

2 tsp baking powder

1 tsp bicarbonate of soda

1½ tsp ground cinnamon

pinch of salt

10 tbsp rolled porridge oats (about 100g), plus extra for sprinkling

15 tbsp (about 200g) berries (frozen or fresh)

handful of seeds (such as pumpkin, sunflower, poppy), to top

1. Preheat the oven to 180°C/160°C fan/Gas Mark 4 and line a 12-hole muffin tin with paper cases.

2. In a jug, whisk together the butter, eggs, yoghurt, honey and vanilla extract.

3. In a large bowl, mix together the flour, baking powder, bicarbonate of soda, cinnamon and salt with the rolled porridge oats.

4. Fold the wet ingredients into the dry ingredients, being careful to not overmix the batter. Finally, fold in the berries. Divide the batter between the 12 muffin cases and top with a few oats and seeds on each.

5. Bake in the oven for 20–25 minutes until golden, risen and a skewer inserted into the middle comes out clean. Pop the paper-cased muffins out of the tin to cool on a wire rack.

FREEZER TO TABLE:
Put a muffin in the microwave on the high setting for 45 seconds–1 minute, or until softened and warmed through (check after every 20-second interval), or wrap in foil and bake in an oven preheated to 200°C/180°C fan/Gas Mark 6 for 5 minutes until hot through. If you want to defrost overnight in the fridge, simply 'refresh' them in the microwave for 10–20 seconds on the high setting.

FREEZE:
Cool the muffins completely before putting into a labelled resealable freezer bag.

Sweetcorn Fritters

MAKES 16 MEDIUM FRITTERS (8 FOR NOW, 8 FOR LATER) • 5 MINUTES PREP • 15 MINUTES COOKING

Best served with a platter of different toppings so everyone can DIT (do-it-themselves) – and it's less work for you, too. A great one for fuzzy heads and hangovers ... bring on the bacon and hot sauce.

4 x 198g tins sweetcorn, drained, or 400g frozen sweetcorn

8 spring onions, finely chopped

8 heaped tbsp flour

4 eggs

4 tsp chopped coriander leaves

4 tsp paprika (sweet or smoked)

12 tbsp milk

oil, for frying

TRY ADDING:
— small handful of crumbled feta
— 1–2 courgettes, grated
— pinch of chilli flakes

1. Put all the ingredients into a large bowl, along with a pinch of salt and pepper and mix well.

2. Heat a tablespoon of oil in a large frying pan over a medium heat. Scoop 1–2 tablespoons of batter into the pan to form one fritter (use a cookie cutter to help keep the batter in a circle shape, if you fancy), cook it for about 5 minutes, turning occasionally, until golden and cooked through (you may need to cook for a few more minutes if you are using frozen sweetcorn). Set aside on a plate lined with kitchen paper. Repeat with the remaining batter and serve.

→ **Try with** crispy bacon, fried eggs, tomato salsa, guacamole, sausages, chopped chillies, sweet chilli sauce.

 FREEZE:
Cool the fritters completely before placing in a labelled resealable freezer bag, with baking parchment separating each fritter.

FREEZER TO TABLE:
Heat the fritters in an oven preheated to 200°C/180°C fan/Gas Mark 6 for 15–20 minutes until piping hot through, then 're-crisp' in a hot pan with a little vegetable oil for a minute or so, flipping over halfway. Or, defrost in the fridge overnight and skip the oven-heating step.

Cinna-berry Pancakes

MAKES 12–16 PANCAKES (6–8 FOR NOW, 6–8 FOR LATER) • 10 MINUTES PREP • 15 MINUTES COOKING

Most mornings my son requests berry pancakes for breakfast. At the weekend it's a no-brainer, but there's really no time for the pancake-making faff (and flour-dusted clothes) during the week, even when he flashes those big peepers at me … So this really is a time-saver/stay in the good books recipe. (Also a clever way to avoid the 'standing over the hob making pancake after pancake for everyone else but yourself' breakfast situation.) Stick with small berries so when you reheat the pancakes you aren't left with cold spots.

300g plain flour

1 tbsp baking powder

2 tsp ground cinnamon

large pinch of salt

2 eggs

500g milk

2 tbsp butter, melted

2 tsp vanilla extract

4 small handfuls of small frozen berries (currants and blueberries are great)

butter, for frying

1. In a large bowl, sift together the flour, baking powder, cinnamon and add the salt.

2. Make a well in the middle of the dry ingredients and break in the eggs, beat it in to make a paste, then whisk in the milk, butter and vanilla until you have a smooth batter. Stir in the berries.

3. Heat a knob of butter in a medium-sized frying pan over a medium heat until frothy, then drop a large tablespoon of batter into the pan, to make a palm-sized pancake. Fry for a few minutes, until the underside is golden and cooked and small bubbles appear on the surface, then flip over and cook for another few minutes until golden and cooked through. You can do a few pancakes at a time. Set aside under a tea towel to keep warm while you finish the rest, then serve.

→ **Try with** Cinna-berry Ice Cube Butter (see page 129), maple syrup, butter, bacon.

 FREEZE:
Cool the pancakes completely and place in a resealable freezer bag, with baking parchment separating each pancake.

 FREEZER TO TABLE:
Heat a little butter in a large frying pan over a low heat. Once melted, place the frozen pancakes in the pan and cook, flipping over regularly, until hot through.

Ice Kitchen Oats

SERVES 8–12 (4–6 FOR NOW AND 4–6 FOR LATER) • 10 MINUTES PREP

Oats are undoubtedly one of the most nutritious and filling ways to start the day. I love porridge, but sometimes when I want something a little more refreshing, overnight oats are the way to go. You can really go to town to make this your own recipe by chopping and changing the dried fruit, spices, nut butters and toppings. I make it in bulk so I can freeze a lot of it for even easier breakfast times. Just remember to put it in the fridge to defrost the night before.

4 heaped tbsp nut butter

8 handfuls of rolled porridge oats

2 handfuls of desiccated coconut

1 tsp grated nutmeg

2 tsp ground cinnamon

pinch of salt

4 handfuls of dried fruit (raisins, dates, apricots, mango, cherries, prunes are all good), roughly chopped

1 litre milk

1. In a large bowl, mix together all the ingredients until well combined. Cover and leave in the fridge overnight.

2. Serve cold with yoghurt, or more milk if you want a runnier consistency, along with fresh fruit and seeds.

→ *Try with* yoghurt, fresh fruit (passionfruit, mango and apple work especially well), nuts, seeds.

❄ *Ice Kitchen Tip*
Freeze leftover cooked porridge in the same way, ensuring it has cooled completely before putting into the muffin tin for flash-freezing. Defrost in the fridge overnight and simply reheat in the microwave (make sure you cover the bowl), or on the hob with additional milk or water. Try adding different flavours to each muffin hole of porridge, such as cocoa powder, coconut or berries.

 FREEZE:
Once the oats have swollen overnight, line the holes of a muffin tin with foil or baking parchment, allowing some overhang at the top. Divide the oats between the muffin holes, cover the tray and flash-freeze in the freezer. Once frozen, use the foil or baking parchment overhang to help pop out the frozen oats and put into a labelled resealable freezer bag.

 FREEZER TO TABLE:
Place a portion in a small bowl, cover with foil or baking parchment and leave in the fridge overnight. Serve as above.

Cheddar French Toast

MAKES 8 SLICES (4 FOR NOW AND 4 FOR LATER) • 15 MINUTES PREP • 10 MINUTES COOKING

The Croque Madame is undeniably the inspiration for this grown-up savoury version of French toast. In my home this is also a go-to light comfort dinner, served with a fried egg on top and a green salad. Any hard cheese can work here, so see what you like best.

8 eggs

4 spring onions, finely chopped

4 tsp chopped chives

20 splashes of Tabasco

2 tbsp Worcestershire sauce

12 tbsp milk

2 tbsp mustard (Dijon or wholegrain)

8 tbsp grated Cheddar or Parmesan cheese

8 slices of good-quality bread

butter, for frying

1. Whisk the eggs with the spring onions, chives, Tabasco, Worcestershire sauce, milk, mustard and cheese, along with some salt and pepper and pour into a wide baking dish.

2. Soak the slices of bread for a minute or so on each side until soft, but don't leave them too long or the bread will start falling apart.

3. Melt the butter in a large frying pan over a medium heat; when it begins to foam, fry the soaked bread slices for a couple of minutes on each side (pouring over any excess soaking liquid) until golden. Serve immediately.

→ **Try with** avocado/guacamole, poached eggs, tomato salsa, smoked salmon, bacon.

❄ *Ice Kitchen Tip*
Freeze sweet versions of French toast in the same way.

 FREEZE:
Cool the Cheddar French Toast completely before putting into a labelled resealable freezer bag, with baking parchment separating each slice.

 FREEZER TO TABLE:
Put the slices on a baking tray and heat in an oven preheated to 200°C/180°C fan/Gas Mark 6 for 5–10 minutes, or until hot through and crispy.

Fridge Forage Frittatas

MAKES 8-10 INDIVIDUAL FRITTATAS (4 FOR NOW, 4-6 FOR LATER) • 10 MINUTES PREP • 30 MINUTES COOKING

Frittatas are a fridge forage saviour in my home – so great for using up odds and ends of ingredients to avoid wasting food, true to *The Ice Kitchen* Method! And this isn't only for breakfast – try it for lunch or dinner (served with a big fresh salad).

2 tbsp oil

2 spring onions, finely chopped

2 garlic cloves, grated or finely chopped

1 tbsp dried thyme

1 tbsp smoked paprika

1 large potato (white or sweet), cut into 1cm cubes

12 cherry tomatoes, halved

8 eggs

2 tbsp crème fraîche

TRY ADDING:

— small handful of any veg (frozen or fresh)

— small handful of ham, chopped, or 2 tsp 'nduja

— small handful of grated or crumbled cheese

SWAP THE DRIED THYME AND SMOKED PAPRIKA FOR:

— *1 tbsp madras curry powder and 1 tbsp coriander leaves*

— *1 tbsp Cajun seasoning*

— *1 tbsp parsley leaves, chopped*

— *1 tbsp basil leaves, chopped*

1. Preheat the oven to 200°C/180°C fan/Gas Mark 6 and grease and line 8-10 ramekins or 8-10 holes of a muffin tin with baking parchment, allowing for some overhang at the top.

2. Heat the oil in a large frying pan over a medium heat and fry the spring onions and garlic with the thyme and smoked paprika until the aroma hits you, about 30 seconds or so.

3. Add the potato, tomato halves and any other vegetables and cook until softened, stirring regularly, for about 10-15 minutes (don't worry if the potato isn't completely cooked through). If you're adding spinach, just add it towards the end of the cooking time, so it cooks just long enough to wilt down. Season with salt and pepper to taste.

4. In a jug, whisk the eggs with the crème fraîche and mix in the ham and cheese along with a pinch of salt and pepper.

5. Divide the vegetable mixture among the ramekins or muffin holes, then carefully pour in the egg mixture. Bake for 20 minutes. Remove from the oven and eat warm, or allow to cool and eat at room temperature, or cold.

 FREEZE:
Cool the frittatas completely, remove them from the ramekins or muffin holes and put into a labelled resealable freezer bag.

 FREEZER TO TABLE:
Wrap in foil and bake in an oven preheated to 200°C/180°C fan/Gas Mark 6 for 20-25 minutes until hot through, or defrost overnight in the fridge and heat in the oven for half the time.

Brown Sugar Banana Bread

SERVES 4 FOR NOW AND 4 FOR LATER • 10 MINUTES PREP • 20 MINUTES COOKING

Ah, the good old banana bread. Usually just a go-to when those bananas are turning black, but now I find myself actually setting aside bananas to overripen so that I can make this gem of a recipe. If I can manage to not finish the whole loaf in a day or so, I slice up the remainder and freeze it so I can pop individual slices in the toaster and have salty-buttered banana bread morning, noon and night!

4 blackened (overripe)
   bananas
200g plain flour, sifted
2½ tsp baking powder
1 tsp salt
150g soft dark brown sugar
2 eggs
5 tbsp melted unsalted
   butter
1 tsp vanilla extract

TRY ADDING:
— handful of nuts (pecans,
   walnuts, hazelnuts,
   macadamia nuts),
   roughly chopped
— handful of chocolate
   chunks or chips (milk,
   white or dark)

1. Preheat the oven to 170°C/150°C fan/Gas Mark 3 and grease a 900g loaf tin.

2. Peel and mash the bananas and set aside.

3. In a small bowl mix together the flour, baking powder and salt.

4. Beat the sugar and eggs together in a large bowl until pale and fluffy, then add the melted butter and vanilla extract and fold in the bananas followed by the dry ingredients. Finally fold in any additional extras, like nuts or chocolate.

5. Pour into the loaf tin and bake in the oven for about 1 hour, or until a skewer comes out clean. Turn out on to a wire rack and leave to cool a bit before serving.

→ *Try with* salted butter, chocolate hazelnut spread, dulce de leche.

FREEZER TO TABLE:
Put individual unwrapped slices into the microwave for 10–20 seconds on the high setting (checking at regular intervals) until softened through, or keep in foil and put the slice on a baking tray into an oven preheated to 170°C/150°C fan/Gas Mark 3 for 5–10 minutes until softened through. You can also pop unwrapped slices into the toaster, keeping a close check that they don't burn! For the whole loaf, keep in foil, put on a baking tray and bake in the oven for 25–35 minutes until softened through.

FREEZE:
Once the bread has cooled completely, slice (not too thickly so it can fit in the toaster) and wrap each piece tightly in foil then pop into a labelled resealable freezer bag (this will stop it drying out). Alternatively, freeze the loaf as a whole (tightly wrap in foil, then pop into a labelled resealable freezer bag), if you fancy.

Ice Kitchen Jam

MAKES ENOUGH TO FILL ABOUT 3 STANDARD JAM JARS • 10 MINUTES PREP • 15 MINUTES COOKING

Who knew you could make jam without having to cook it?! This soft-set beauty is so simple and just perfect for a mass of berries that are slightly past it. You can flavour it with spices or even herbs (try a little basil!) and then slather it on toast and crumpets, use it to top creamy puds like rice pudding (see page 163), swirl through your No Churn Ice Cream (see page 168) or add it to ice lollies such as the popsicles (see page 177). If you can find mini jars or freezerproof containers I would suggest using these to store this jam. That way you can take out smaller portions and not need to use it all up in 3 weeks.

500g berries, fresh or
  defrosted if frozen
500g jam sugar
1 tsp vanilla extract
2 tbsp fresh lemon juice

TRY ADDING:
— 1 tsp ground cinnamon
— ½ tsp ground allspice
— ½ tsp ground ginger
— 1½ tsp finely chopped
  basil leaves

1. Roughly crush the fruit in a large bowl, then add the sugar, vanilla and lemon juice and stir well for about 3 minutes until properly combined. Ladle the mixture into a jug and then pour into the clean jam jars or small freezerproof containers with lids (for example, small Tupperware, or resealable freezerproof bags). Be sure to leave about an inch of space at the top of the jar or container (if using mini jars or containers, you can halve this) for the jam to expand as it freezes. Put the lids on and leave out at room temperature for 24 hours.

 FREEZE:
Simply put the labelled containers into the freezer.

 FREEZER TO TABLE:
Take the jam out and defrost at room temperature about an hour before you want to use it. Store in the fridge after it has defrosted and use within 3 weeks.

Sweet Potato & Chorizo Hash

SERVES 8 (4 FOR NOW AND 4 FOR LATER) • 15 MINUTES PREP • 25 MINUTES COOKING

Another brunch stalwart, but just as delicious at other times too. There is something truly 'meant to be' about this sweet potato, chorizo and smoked paprika combo. What is it they say? Never mess with a classic? When frozen flat, I find I can easily break off a chunk of just the right amount – perfect when it's just me, myself and I.

4 large sweet potatoes, unpeeled and cut into 1cm cubes

4 heaped tbsp butter

4 large onions, sliced

3 garlic cloves, grated or finely chopped

2 tbsp smoked paprika

2 tbsp dried thyme, or 4 sprigs of fresh thyme, leaves chopped

1–2 tsp cayenne pepper

2 dry-cured chorizo rings, diced

2 large handfuls of spinach, or 4–6 cubes of frozen spinach, defrosted

1. Parboil the sweet potatoes for 5 minutes, drain then leave to dry.

2. Put the butter into a large frying pan set over a medium heat; when it starts to foam, add the onions with a generous pinch of salt and soften for 5 minutes.

3. Add the garlic, smoked paprika, thyme, cayenne pepper and chorizo and cook for about 5 minutes, stirring often.

4. Add the sweet potato and stir to combine, then cook for 10–15 minutes, squashing with a fish slice to allow the skin to crust up a bit before flipping over and repeating.

5. Add the spinach and cook for 5 more minutes, stirring now and again. Season with salt and pepper to taste, then serve.

→ **Try with** fried eggs, fresh parsley, chopped chillies, chopped spring onions.

FREEZER TO TABLE:
Empty the hash into an ovenproof dish, cover with foil and heat in an oven preheated to 200°C/180°C fan/Gas Mark 6 for 20–25 minutes, removing the foil for the last 5 minutes, until hot through. Or, defrost overnight in the fridge and heat in the oven for half the time.

FREEZE:
Cool completely and freeze flat (spreading the hash out into one layer) in a resealable freezer bag (use two bags if necessary). Or portion out and freeze individually.

Breakfast Beans

SERVES 8 (4 FOR NOW AND 4 FOR LATER) • 5 MINUTES PREP • 20 MINUTES COOKING

Who remembers those tins of beans packed with mini sausages? That was the inspiration for this handy recipe, which is essentially half a fry-up ... just add the eggs and some toast. Add a little chilli powder if you want a bit of a kick. Definitely one of those to whip out at the weekend to save on the washing up.

6 sausages, or 12 chipolata sausages (or use vegetarian sausages)

24 rashers of streaky bacon

2 tbsp oil

2 garlic cloves, grated or finely chopped

4 tsp dried thyme

4 tsp smoked paprika

4 x 400g tins cannellini beans, drained

2 x 400g tins chopped tomatoes

4 tbsp soft dark brown sugar

TRY ADDING:

— handful of sliced/torn mushrooms

— handful of spinach (stir in near the end of cooking to just wilt)

1. Preheat the oven to 200°C/180°C fan/Gas Mark 6. Put the sausages and bacon on a baking tray and cook for about 20 minutes until cooked and crisp, then remove and set aside.

2. Heat the oil in a large saucepan over a medium heat and fry the garlic and spices, stirring until the aroma hits you, about 30 seconds or so.

3. Add the beans, tomatoes and brown sugar (and mushrooms, if using) and increase the heat to bring up to the boil. Reduce the heat to low and simmer until thickened, about 10–15 minutes. Season with salt and pepper to taste.

4. Chop the sausages and bacon rashers into bite-size pieces, stir into the beans and serve.

➔ **Try with** eggs, buttered toast, hash browns and other fry-up bits and bobs.

 FREEZE:
Cool completely and freeze flat (spreading the beans out into a thin layer) in a labelled resealable freezer bag, dividing between two or more bags if necessary, before filing upright.

 FREEZER TO TABLE:
Empty into a lidded saucepan, over a low-medium heat, breaking it up as it defrosts. When fully defrosted, add a splash of water, increase the heat and cook, stirring often, until piping hot through. Or defrost overnight in the fridge, before reheating on the hob.

Main Meals

These are meals that can go from freezer to table without much extra thought, save possibly cooking a bit of rice or putting together a salad. But for the most part you can change into your cosies, put your feet up and unwind while your meal is being heated courtesy of that oven or hob! I've divided this chapter into the time it takes to make the original recipe from first chop to table, for ease of reference ... and so you can make decisions depending on how *hangry* you are ...

QUICK (30 MINUTES OR LESS)
Creole Gumbo
Feta Spinach Filo Pie
Lentil Chilli Non-Carne
Coconut Prawn Curry
Pineapple Fried Coconut Rice
Sausage & Lentil Hotpot
Curried Fish Pie
Eastern Stuffed Peppers
Jerked Mac 'N' Cheese
Gazpacho
Quick Savoury Puff Tart

MEDIUM (45 MINUTES OR LESS)
Peanut Stew
Indian Spiced Beans
Ginger & Turmeric Dal
Pineapple Chicken Enchiladas
Butternut Squash & Sage Pasta Bake
Vegetable Toad in the Hole
Onion Gravy
Freezer Pizza
Carrot & Coriander Soup
Minestrone
Spanish Seafood Stew

LONGER (45 MINUTES PLUS)
North African Chicken Traybake
Beef & Prune Tagine
Beef Rendang
Chipotle Pulled Pork
Meatloaf
Sticky Ribs
Ratatouille
Cheat's Jamaican Beef Patties
Katsu Curry

Creole Gumbo

SERVES 8 (4 FOR NOW AND 4 FOR LATER) • 10 MINUTES PREP • 20 MINUTES COOKING

Gumbo is a real one-pot wonder, brim-full of a glorious combination of ingredients. This makes a fantastic lazy weekend lunch centrepiece, to keep revisiting over the course of the afternoon. It's another one of those dishes that tastes even more incredible from the freezer a few weeks later.

2 glugs of oil

4 skinless chicken breasts, or 8 skinless thighs, chopped into large chunks

400g smoked sausage, or chorizo, sliced

2 large onions, finely chopped

4 celery sticks, finely chopped

2 green peppers, deseeded and finely chopped

5 garlic cloves, finely chopped

3 tbsp Cajun seasoning

4 sprigs of thyme

2 heaped tbsp flour

1 litre chicken stock

2 x 400g tins chopped tomatoes

2 x 175g packs okra, topped and tailed, sliced into 1cm pieces

400g frozen raw prawns

SWAP THE CHICKEN OR PRAWNS FOR:

— cubed sweet potato

— sweetcorn cobetttes (or frozen sweetcorn)

1. Heat the oil in a large saucepan over a medium heat, then add the chicken and sausage. Brown on all sides, remove and set aside.

2. Add a little more oil if needed and add the onions, celery and green peppers. Fry for 5–10 minutes, stirring regularly until softened. Add the garlic, Cajun seasoning and thyme and stir continuously until the aroma hits you, about 20 seconds or so.

3. Return the chicken and sausage, along with any juices, back to the pan. Add the flour and stir to coat all the contents of the pot. Add the stock, chopped tomatoes and okra, increase the heat to bring up to the boil, then reduce the heat to low and simmer with the lid on, for 15–20 minutes until cooked. Season with salt and pepper to taste. If you're not planning to freeze, add the prawns now and heat for a couple more minutes until they are just cooked.

→ **Try with** rice, cornbread, lime wedges and sliced spring onion.

 FREEZE:
Cool completely, then portion up (I like preparing portions of two) and place into labelled resealable freezer bags. Lay flat to freeze, before filing upright.

FREEZER TO TABLE:
Empty into a lidded saucepan and place over a low-medium heat, breaking it up as it defrosts. Once fully defrosted, add a splash of water, increase the heat and cook, stirring often, until piping hot. Add the prawns at the last moment and cook for a couple of minutes. Or defrost overnight in the fridge, before reheating on the hob.

Feta Spinach Filo Pie

SERVES 8 (4 FOR NOW AND 4 FOR LATER) • 15 MINUTES PREP • 20 MINUTES COOKING

This spanakopita-inspired dish is perfect for showcasing filo's flaky perfection and seems to be quite enjoyable to even most regular spinach-haters. A great reason to keep filo at close reach in your Ice Kitchen. You can freeze the uncooked pie – but if you do, make sure you use fresh (previously unfrozen) filo for this!

2 tbsp olive oil, plus extra
  for brushing
2 leeks, thinly sliced
8 spring onions, thinly sliced
500g spinach (fresh or
  defrosted)
2 blocks of feta cheese,
  crumbled
8 sheets of filo pastry
  (previously unfrozen)

TRY ADDING:
— chopped sundried
  tomatoes at step 3

1. Preheat the oven to 200°C/180°C fan/Gas Mark 6.

2. Heat the oil in a large frying pan over a medium heat, then add the leeks and spring onions, stirring occasionally until softened, about 10 minutes.

3. Blanch the spinach briefly in just-boiled water, so it wilts. When cool, squeeze out any excess water. Mix the spinach with the feta and the softened leek and spring onion, then season with salt and pepper to taste.

4. Layer 2 sheets of filo pastry into one of two 20 x 25cm baking dishes. Halve the filling and pour out on to the pastry in one dish, spread out and then fold the filo over. Then layer two more sheets on top, tuck the edges in and brush with a little oil. Bake in the oven for 15–20 minutes until golden brown. Eat hot or cold.

→ *Try with* a fresh salad.

❋ *Ice Kitchen Tip*
Never defrost filled filo pastry pies as they will become soggy; instead cook from frozen in a preheated oven.

FREEZE:
At step 4, line the other baking dish with foil with some overhang, then assemble the pie as above but don't brush it with oil and don't bake it. Wrap the pie and put into the freezer until frozen, then use the foil to remove the pie from the dish. Wrap well in more foil, then put into a labelled resealable freezer bag and put into the freezer.

FREEZER TO TABLE:
Unwrap the pie and put back into the baking dish. Brush the top with a little oil, cover with foil, then bake in a preheated oven as above for about 30 minutes, removing the foil for the last 15–20 minutes, until piping hot through and golden brown.

Lentil Chilli Non-Carne

SERVES 8 (4 FOR NOW AND 4 FOR LATER) • 10 MINUTES PREP • 20 MINUTES COOKING

One of my fondest childhood meal memories was my Pa's chilli, devoured in seconds by my ravenous sisters, Rhe and Ash, and always eaten with spiced potato wedges. I made a vegetarian version to switch it up a bit and to cut down on my meat intake. As delicious as ever!

1 tbsp oil

2 large onions, finely chopped

2 large carrots, finely diced

5 garlic cloves, finely chopped

1 tbsp ground cumin

1 tbsp ground coriander

¼–1 tsp chilli powder, depending on how hot you like it

4 x 400g tins green lentils, drained

2 x 400g tins kidney beans, drained

2 x 400g tins chopped tomatoes

2 vegetable stock cubes, crumbled

1. Heat the oil in a large saucepan over a medium heat, then add the onions and carrots and cook, stirring regularly, until slightly softened, about 5 minutes. Add the garlic and spices and stir for 30 seconds or so until the aroma hits.

2. Add the remaining ingredients, along with a tinful (using one of the empty tins) of water. Increase the heat, bring up to the boil, then reduce the heat to low and let the chilli simmer for 20–30 minutes until thick. Season with salt and pepper to taste and serve.

→ **Try with** white rice, fresh coriander, tortilla chips, or Pa's way: with potato wedges!

 FREEZE:
Cool completely, then portion up (I like preparing portions of two) and pour into labelled resealable freezer bags. Lay the chilli flat until frozen, then file upright in your freezer.

 FREEZER TO TABLE:
Empty into a lidded saucepan and place over a low-medium heat, breaking it up as it defrosts. Once fully defrosted, add a splash of water, increase the heat and cook, stirring often, until piping hot through. Or defrost overnight in the fridge before reheating on the hob.

Coconut Prawn Curry

SERVES 8 (4 FOR NOW AND 4 FOR LATER) • 10 MINUTES PREP • 25 MINUTES COOKING

This recipe is based on a dish you might eat at a beachfront restaurant somewhere like Store Bay in Tobago; after getting your hands messy you go rinse them (and the rest of you) off in the bathwater-warm sea. An effortless but impressive recipe – the epitome of Ice Kitchen freezer food ...

a glug of oil
2 onions, finely chopped
5 garlic cloves, finely chopped
2.cm piece of ginger, peeled and grated
3 tbsp garam masala
2 tbsp ground turmeric
2 x 400ml tins coconut milk
2 x 400g tins chopped tomatoes
1–1.2kg frozen raw jumbo king prawns, ideally shell on

SWAP THE PRAWNS FOR:

— *fruits de mer*
— *chunks of meaty fish (frozen or fresh)*

1. Heat the oil in a large saucepan over a medium heat, then add the onions, stirring regularly until softened, about 10 minutes. Add the garlic, ginger and spices, stirring continuously until the aromas hit you, about 20 seconds or so.

2. Add the coconut milk and chopped tomatoes, increase the heat to bring to the boil then reduce the heat to low. If you're adding chunks of fish, add them to the pan now and simmer for about 15 minutes, or until the sauce is thickened. Season with salt and pepper to taste.

3. Remove half the sauce for freezing For Later.

4. Add the prawns to the saucepan and cook for a few minutes, until just cooked, then serve.

→ ***Try with*** fragrant rice, flatbreads (see page 135), wedges of lime and fresh coriander.

FREEZE:
Follow the recipe up to the end of step 2. Allow to cool completely before pouring into labelled resealable freezer bags (I like preparing portions of two). Lay flat to freeze, then file upright.

FREEZER TO TABLE:
Empty into a lidded saucepan and place over a low-medium heat, breaking it up as it defrosts. Once fully defrosted, add a splash of water, increase the heat and cook, stirring often, until piping hot through, then add the frozen prawns and cook for a few minutes until the prawns are just cooked. Or defrost overnight in the fridge, before reheating on the hob.

Pineapple Fried Coconut Rice

SERVES 8 (4 FOR NOW AND 4 FOR LATER) • 10 MINUTES PREP • 25 MINUTES COOKING

Could this sound any more tropical? I love food that is as colourful as a rainbow and so full of different textures and flavours. While it is a wonderful meal in its own right, it is also a brilliant addition to grilled meats and fish. A midweek magic meal!

600g long-grain rice

4 large glugs of vegetable oil

2 large garlic cloves, smashed

1 tsp ground allspice

4 sprigs of thyme

2 x 400ml tins coconut milk

8 spring onions, thinly sliced

2 small chillies, finely chopped

2 x 325g tins sweetcorn, drained (or use 500g frozen)

2 x 220g tins pineapple chunks, drained

6 tbsp finely chopped coriander

a couple of large handfuls of unsalted cashew nuts, chopped

TRY ADDING:

— beans (kidney, black, pinto, mixed) at step 3

— strips of chicken or pork at step 3 - just make sure it is cooked and piping hot through

1. Rinse the rice in a sieve under cold running water. Heat a large glug of oil in a large saucepan over a medium heat and add the garlic, allspice, thyme and drained rice. Stir well to coat the rice.

2. Add 400ml water and bring to the boil, then add the coconut milk, reduce the heat and simmer until the rice is cooked, about 15–20 minutes.

3. Carefully remove the garlic clove and thyme and set aside. Heat another large glug of oil in a large frying pan or wok over a high heat, then fry the garlic clove, thyme, spring onions and chillies, stirring continuously, until the aromas hit you, for 30 seconds or so. Then add the sweetcorn, pineapple and coriander and continue to fry for another 5 minutes (you may need a few minutes extra if using frozen sweetcorn), stirring continuously. Finally add in the rice, give it a quick stir so everything is well mixed through and season with salt and pepper to taste. Set aside half for freezing and add the cashew nuts into the other half, frying for another minute or so, stirring continuously, and serve.

 FREEZER TO TABLE:
Empty portions into a microwaveable bowl, cover and microwave in bursts on the defrost setting, checking every few minutes or so, until defrosted. Or, add the frozen rice to a large frying pan along with a splash of water. Cover and cook over a low heat, stirring now and again, until the rice is defrosted. Just before serving, heat a little oil in a wok over a high heat, add the rice and fry quickly, adding the cashew nuts for the last minute or so, until piping hot. Or defrost overnight in the fridge, before reheating as above.

FREEZE:
Leave the cashew nuts out of the recipe and allow the rice to completely cool, then portion up (I like preparing portions of two) and place into a labelled resealable freezer bag. Lay flat to freeze, before filing upright.

Sausage & Lentil Hotpot

SERVES 8 (4 FOR NOW AND 4 FOR LATER) • 10 MINUTES PREP • 30 MINUTES COOKING

I can't write a book of freezer recipes without featuring the humble but heavenly sausage, an Ice Kitchen stalwart. My favourite way to enjoy a sausage is in a stew or casserole; this particular recipe throws them into an earthy background of herbs, mushrooms and lentils. Perfect fodder for a quick comfort feast.

2 glugs of oil

24 sausages (use vegetarian, if you like)

2 large onions, finely chopped

2 red peppers, deseeded and roughly chopped

3 large garlic cloves, grated or finely chopped

2 large sprigs of rosemary

4 large sprigs of thyme

1 litre vegetable or chicken stock

4 tbsp tomato purée

6 handfuls of button or other mushrooms (about 300g), torn or roughly chopped

2 x 400g tins lentils (green, brown or puy)

SWAP THE ROSEMARY FOR:

— *2 tbsp smoked paprika*

— *1 tsp chilli powder*

— *2 large handfuls of black olives*

1. Heat the oil in a large saucepan over a high heat and add the sausages. Cook them until browned, then carefully remove them and set aside. Reduce the heat to medium, add the onion and pepper and cook, stirring regularly, until softened, about 5 minutes.

2. Add the garlic, rosemary and thyme and stir continuously until the aroma is released, for 20 seconds or so. Add the stock, tomato purée, mushrooms, lentils and sausages. Increase the heat, bring up to the boil, then reduce the heat and simmer over a medium heat for about 20 minutes, stirring often, until the sausages are cooked through. Season with salt and pepper to taste and serve.

→ **Try with** creamy mashed potato.

 FREEZE:
Cool completely, then portion up (I like preparing portions of two) into labelled resealable freezer bags and lay flat to freeze, before filing upright.

FREEZER TO TABLE:
Empty into an ovenproof dish, cover with foil and bake for 45 minutes–1 hour in an oven preheated to 200°C/180°C fan/Gas Mark 6 until piping hot through. Or defrost in the fridge overnight, then place in a saucepan, add a splash of water, cover with a lid and heat over a medium heat until piping hot through.

Curried Fish Pie

SERVES 8 (4 FOR NOW AND 4 FOR LATER) • 10 MINUTES PREP • 25 MINUTES COOKING

A lovely little twist on a favourite that every household must have ready-to-go in the freezer; even fish naysayers seem to love this one. I personally love making individual ramekins of this, like finding pots of gold in the icy depths. You can also always remove the curry powder for a more classic flavour. You can also use fresh fish – just reduce the cooking time in step 3, until just cooked.

a couple of glugs of oil, plus extra for drizzling

2 onions, chopped

3 garlic cloves, grated

4 tbsp medium madras curry powder

½ tsp grated nutmeg

2 tbsp finely chopped parsley

2 tbsp butter

2 heaped tbsp flour

570ml whole milk

selection of greens (e.g. a handful of broccoli florets, a couple of large handfuls of frozen peas or spinach, or a mix)

juice of 1 lemon

about 600–800g frozen fish pie mix

5 medium potatoes (about 1kg), peeled, boiled and mashed with large knob of butter and seasoning

1. Preheat the oven to 200°C/180°C fan/Gas Mark 6.

2. Heat the oil in a large saucepan over a medium heat, then add the onions, stirring regularly until softened, about 5 minutes. Add the garlic, curry powder, nutmeg and parsley, stirring continuously until the aroma hits you, for 20 seconds or so.

3. Add the butter and flour and whisk until there is no dry flour left. Whisk in the milk, increase the heat and thicken the sauce for about 5 minutes, stirring regularly. Reduce the heat to medium and add the greens, lemon juice and fish pie mix, cover with a lid and cook for 10–15 minutes until the vegetables, fish and seafood are just cooked through. If you want the sauce a little thicker, remove the lid while it cooks. Season with salt and pepper to taste.

4. Pour half of the filling into a deep baking dish (around 25 x 20cm), or divide among individual ramekins. Top with the mashed potato and a drizzle of oil. Bake in the oven for 15 minutes until golden and bubbling and serve.

 FREEZE:
Before filling the other baking dish, line it with foil, with some overhang. Pour the filling into the dish, top with the mashed potato and allow to cool completely. Cover the dish with foil and put into the freezer; once frozen solid, lift out, wrap in more foil and store in the freezer in a labelled resealable freezer bag. Or portion into individual ramekins, covered with foil, and place in the freezer.

 FREEZER TO TABLE:
Unwrap the whole pie and place back in the baking dish, covered in foil. Bake in an oven preheated to 200°C/180°C fan/Gas Mark 6 for 30–45 minutes until piping hot through, uncovering for the final 5 minutes. Cook individual ramekins for 25–30 minutes. Or defrost overnight in the fridge and halve the oven timings, then pop under a hot grill for a few minutes until bubbling and burnished.

Eastern Stuffed Peppers

SERVES 8 (4 FOR NOW AND 4 FOR LATER) • 10 MINUTES PREP • 20 MINUTES COOKING

This is just perfect for a summer's day with a glass of something crisp and cold. The fresh flavours, varying textures and kick of mint and heat really sing through to make a wondrously refreshing meal. A great dish to have up your sleeves and a perfect example of how *The Ice Kitchen* Method of cooking and eating can be light and fresh as well as pure comfort.

8 peppers (red, orange, or yellow), halved and deseeded

4 tbsp raisins

4 tbsp black olives, sliced

4 tbsp sundried tomatoes, finely chopped

4 tbsp finely chopped parsley leaves

4 tbsp finely chopped mint leaves

4 tsp Aleppo pepper flakes

400g couscous, prepared in stock, as per the packet instructions

2 blocks of halloumi, cut into 16 thin slices

4 tbsp toasted pine nuts

extra-virgin olive oil, for drizzling

1. Preheat the oven to 200°C/180°C fan/Gas Mark 6.

2. Put the pepper halves in the microwave on high for 5–10 minutes until a little softened.

3. In a bowl, mix together the raisins, black olives, sundried tomatoes, most of the herbs and Aleppo pepper flakes, then fold in the couscous. Season with salt and pepper to taste.

4. Fill the pepper halves with the couscous mixture. Place half of the peppers on a baking tray and top each stuffed pepper half with halloumi. Bake for about 10 minutes. Set aside the other stuffed halves.

5. Put the peppers under a hot grill for a few minutes until the halloumi is golden and a little melted.

6. Sprinkle over the pine nuts and reserved herbs and drizzle over the extra-virgin olive oil.

FREEZE:
Follow the instructions up to step 4. Let the For Later stuffed peppers cool completely, then wrap well in foil, put into a labelled resealable freezer bag and freeze.

FREEZER TO TABLE:
Put the foil-covered peppers into the oven and bake for 25–35 minutes in an oven preheated to 200°C/180°C fan/Gas Mark 6 until piping hot through, uncovering for the final 5 minutes. Top with the halloumi and grill under a hot grill for a few minutes, until golden and a little melted, then add the pine nuts and the drizzle of olive oil, as above. Or defrost overnight in the fridge and halve the oven timings.

Jerked Mac 'N' Cheese

SERVES 8–12 (4–6 FOR NOW AND 4–6 FOR LATER) • 10 MINUTES PREP • 25 MINUTES COOKING

Mac 'n' cheese is universally touted as one of the most comforting of the comfort foods. It also happens to be an incredible base for so many different flavours and ingredient combos. One of my favourite ways to give it a twist is by simply adding some jerk marinade or sauce, giving it a good kick with a bit of a tropical vibe.

6 tbsp butter, plus extra for the topping

4 tbsp plain flour

6 spring onions, finely chopped

6 garlic cloves, crushed

2 litres milk

6 large handfuls (about 400g) of grated mature Cheddar cheese

2 large handfuls of grated Parmesan cheese, plus 6 tbsp extra for the topping

4–6 cubes Jerk Marinade (see page 126), or use a shop-bought jerk sauce

2 x 400g tins kidney beans, drained

1kg macaroni, cooked as per the packet instructions and drained

12 tbsp breadcrumbs

1. Preheat the grill to high.

2. Melt the 6 tablespoons of butter in a large saucepan over a low heat, then add the flour, increase the heat to medium and whisk continuously until you have a paste. Add the spring onions and garlic and whisk continuously for a couple more minutes. Gradually whisk in the milk until the mixture is smooth. Bring to the boil, then reduce to a simmer, whisking occasionally, until thickened and smooth, about 10–15 minutes.

3. Stir in the cheese along with the jerk marinade, kidney beans and drained pasta. Stir until well combined, then season with salt and pepper to taste. Halve the mixture and pour the For Now portion into a large, wide, baking dish, and the For Later portion into a foil-lined baking dish (with overhang).

4. Melt a knob of butter in a frying pan over a low heat and mix in the breadcrumbs and reserved Parmesan. Spread this evenly over the top of the two dishes, then pop both under the grill for about 5 minutes until bubbling and burnished. Serve immediately.

FREEZE:
After grilling, and once it is completely cool, you can put the whole dish, covered, into the freezer to flash-freeze, then lift out the frozen mac 'n' cheese from the dish to store it whole. Place in a labelled resealable freezer bag or wrap well in more foil.

FREEZER TO TABLE:
Unwrap and place in a baking dish, covered in foil, then bake in an oven preheated to 180°C/160°C fan/Gas Mark 4 for 45–60 minutes until piping hot through, uncovering for the final 5 minutes. Or defrost overnight in the fridge and halve the oven timings. Pop under a hot grill for a few minutes until bubbling and burnished.

Gazpacho

SERVES 8–12 (4–6 FOR NOW AND 4–6 FOR LATER) • 15 MINUTES PREP • 30 MINUTES WAITING

The perfect recipe for balmy summers and stale bread, but it is definitely worth getting some good-quality and beautifully fragrant tomatoes. I like to serve this up with a platter of different toppings so each diner can tailor their soup to their tastes.

1 stale white crusty baguette, or ½ sourdough loaf, torn into small pieces

2kg ripe vine tomatoes, diced

2 medium cucumbers, peeled and diced

2 green peppers, deseeded and diced

3 garlic cloves, finely chopped

4 tbsp sherry vinegar

8 tbsp extra-virgin olive oil

1. Place the bread into a large bowl, then scatter over the diced tomato, cucumber and pepper, followed by the garlic, sherry vinegar and extra-virgin olive oil. Give it a good stir and leave for 30 minutes.

2. Blitz in a food processor or blender until smooth. Season with salt and pepper to taste and serve cold.

➔ **Try with** crumbled feta and shredded mint leaves, or a chopped hard-boiled egg.

 FREEZE:
Portion up in labelled resealable freezer bags and lay flat to freeze until solid, then file upright.

 FREEZER TO TABLE:
Defrost in the fridge or at room temperature. Can be eaten as soon as it has fully defrosted. It may need a quick blitz with a handheld blender, to make the consistency even.

Quick Savoury Puff Tart

SERVES 8 (4 FOR NOW AND 4 FOR LATER) • 15 MINUTES PREP • 15 MINUTES COOKING

Another testament to puff pastry perfection. I prepare the pastry sheet then scavenge the fridge to peg together my toppings. Great for random bits and bobs in your fridge, like feta or olives, and perfect to tailor to fussy-eaters. Don't worry about exact quantities, just make sure your tarts are laden with delicious toppings of your choice.

2 ready-rolled (previously unfrozen) sheets of puff pastry, or 2 packets of (previously unfrozen) puff pastry rolled out to a thickness of 5mm

1 egg, beaten, to glaze

TOPPING IDEAS

— crumbled goat's cheese and caramelised onions
— sundried tomatoes, pesto, mozzarella and basil
— olives, feta, balsamic glaze and thin courgette ribbons
— Brie, cooked roasted sweet potato, cranberry sauce and thyme
— cooked mushroom and taleggio cheese
— cooked flaked salmon mixed with crème fraîche and mustard and cooked asparagus

1. Preheat the oven to 220°C/200°C fan/Gas Mark 7.

2. Open up the puff pastry sheets, fold over the edges of the pastry to make a 1.5cm border and brush the border of one of the sheets with beaten egg.

3. Add your toppings and bake the egg-washed sheet for 15–20 minutes until the pastry is golden and risen at the edges.

 FREEZE:
Follow the recipe up to step 2, add your toppings, but don't brush the border with beaten egg. Put on to a tray lined with baking parchment and flash-freeze. Once frozen solid, wrap in foil, label up and put into your freezer file.

FREEZER TO TABLE:
Preheat the oven to 220°C/200°C fan/Gas Mark 7 and put a baking sheet inside. Unwrap the tart, brush the border with beaten egg, put on the preheated tray and bake for 20–25 minutes until the pastry is puffed up and golden.

Peanut Stew

SERVES 8 (4 FOR NOW AND 4 FOR LATER) • 10 MINUTES PREP • 30 MINUTES COOKING

When I feel like I need a boost of my five-a-day, this is the heart-warming, earthy, rainbow-veg meal I tend to root for. And so comforting. Make sure you serve it with the lime and some hot sauce for the ultimate meal.

glug of oil

2 onions, finely chopped

2 red peppers, deseeded and roughly chopped

5 large garlic cloves, grated

2.5cm piece of ginger, peeled and finely chopped

2 tbsp ground coriander

1 tbsp ground cumin

6 heaped tbsp smooth peanut butter

1 litre vegetable stock

4 medium sweet potatoes, chopped into bite-size chunks

2 x 400g tins chickpeas, drained

2 small bags of spinach (about 80g), or 4–6 cubes frozen spinach

1. Heat the oil in a large saucepan over a medium heat, then add the onion and peppers, stirring regularly until softened, about 5 minutes.

2. Add the garlic, ginger and spices and stir continuously, until the aromas hit you, for 20 seconds or so.

3. Add the peanut butter and stock, stirring until well mixed, then add the sweet potatoes and chickpeas and cook, with the lid on, for about 25 minutes until the sweet potato is cooked through. Add the spinach towards the end of the cooking time, so it just wilts down. Season with salt and pepper to taste and serve.

→ *Try with* cooked rice, fresh bird's-eye chillies or peri-peri sauce, fresh coriander, wedges of lime.

❊ *Ice Kitchen Tip*
Any leftover stock can be frozen in ice-cube trays (covered), then popped into a labelled resealable freezer bag.

FREEZE:
Cool completely, then portion up (I like preparing portions of two) and pour into labelled resealable freezer bags. Lay flat to freeze, then file upright.

FREEZER TO TABLE:
Empty into a lidded saucepan and place over a low-medium heat, breaking it up as it defrosts. Once fully defrosted, add a splash of water, increase the heat and cook, stirring often, until piping hot through. Or defrost overnight in the fridge before reheating on the hob.

Indian Spiced Beans

SERVES 8 (4 FOR NOW AND 4 FOR LATER) • 10 MINUTES PREP • 35 MINUTES COOKING

Very, very lightly inspired by one of my absolute favourite dishes, black dal makhani, a bowlful of these warming, sweet spiced beans will rejuvenate any spirit. If ever I fancy an Indian takeout midweek, this is what I take out of my freezer instead: all the flavour, less expense and ready in less time than it takes for the delivery guy to arrive!

2 tbsp ghee, or butter

2 small onions, roughly chopped

5 large garlic cloves, grated or finely chopped

2.5cm piece of fresh ginger, peeled and grated

2 tbsp ground cardamom

2 tbsp garam masala

1 tsp ground cinnamon

2 x 400g tins chopped tomatoes

2 x 400g tins kidney beans, drained

2 x 400g tins black beans, drained

6 heaped tbsp natural yoghurt (or use double cream)

TRY ADDING:

— 1 tsp dried chillies for extra heat

1. Heat the ghee or butter in a large saucepan over a low heat, then add the onions, stirring regularly until softened, about 5 minutes.

2. Add the garlic, ginger and spices and stir continuously, until the aromas hit you, for 20 seconds or so.

3. Add the tomatoes, kidney beans, black beans and yoghurt or cream. Give it a good stir, put the lid on and simmer for 30 minutes. Carefully use a hand blender to blitz briefly, leaving the beans a little chunky. Season with salt and pepper to taste and serve.

→ **Try with** cooked rice, flatbreads (see page 135) and freshly chopped coriander leaves.

 FREEZE:
Cool completely, then portion up (I like preparing portions of two) and pour into labelled resealable freezer bags. Lay flat (spreading the beans into a single layer) to freeze, then file upright.

FREEZER TO TABLE:
Empty into a lidded saucepan and place over a low-medium heat, breaking it up as it defrosts. Once fully defrosted, add a splash of water, increase the heat and cook, stirring often, until piping hot through. Or defrost overnight in the fridge before reheating on the hob.

Ginger & Turmeric Dal

SERVES 8 (4 FOR NOW AND 4 FOR LATER) • 10 MINUTES PREP • 40 MINUTES COOKING

This dal is pure sunshine and I swear that it works some kind of magic from the inside out (especially good for breaking out during the sniffles season). Truly one of those dishes that simply tastes better and better with time. Such Ice Kitchen gold!

500g red split lentils

2 tbsp ghee or butter

2 onions, finely chopped

4 garlic cloves, finely chopped

2.5cm piece of fresh ginger, peeled and finely chopped

2 tsp ground turmeric

2 tsp ground coriander

2 x 400g tins chopped tomatoes

6 handfuls of spinach, or 6–8 cubes of frozen spinach

1. Put the lentils into a small saucepan, along with 1 litre water. Bring to the boil, reduce the heat and simmer for 20 minutes until the lentils are cooked through. Drain.

2. Heat the ghee or butter in a saucepan over a medium heat and fry the onion for 10–15 minutes, stirring often, until golden brown. Add the garlic, ginger and spices and stir continuously, until the aromas hit you, for a minute or so.

3. Add the chopped tomatoes along with the cooked lentils, cover with a lid and simmer for 10 minutes. Add the spinach for the last couple of minutes, or if using frozen, add it at the same time as the lentils. Season with salt and pepper to taste and serve.

→ **Try with** cooked rice and flatbreads (see page 135).

❋ *Ice Kitchen Tip*
Any leftover ginger can be peeled, grated and portioned in ice-cube trays (covered) and then frozen. Once solid, pop into a labelled resealable freezer bag.

 FREEZE:
Cool completely, then portion up (I like preparing portions of two) and pour into labelled resealable freezer bags. Lay flat (spread the dal out in a single layer) to freeze.

FREEZER TO TABLE:
Empty into a lidded saucepan and place over a low-medium heat, breaking it up as it defrosts. Once fully defrosted, add a splash of water, increase the heat and cook, stirring often, until piping hot through. Or defrost overnight in the fridge, before reheating on the hob.

Pineapple Chicken Enchiladas

SERVES 8 (4 FOR NOW AND 4 FOR LATER) • 15 MINUTES PREP • 45 MINUTES COOKING

Enchiladas are a perfect canvas in which to throw all your fridge-foraged ingredients, so get creative. This particular recipe of sweet pineapple, earthy spice and chilli works so magically.

2 glugs of oil

2 large onions, thinly sliced

4 large peppers (a mix of red, orange, or yellow), deseeded and thinly sliced

3 large garlic cloves, finely chopped

2 tbsp ground cumin

2 tbsp dried oregano

2 tbsp smoked paprika

½–2 tsp chilli powder (depending on how hot you like it!)

about 800g chicken breast mini fillets (straight from frozen is fine too; see page 104)

2 x 400g tins chopped tomatoes

about 400g small pineapple chunks (tinned or fresh)

16 tortilla wraps

6 handfuls of grated Cheddar cheese

SWAP THE CHICKEN FOR:

— *strips of pork*

TRY ADDING:

— cubed sweet potato

— tinned black beans or refried beans

— tinned or frozen sweetcorn

— handful of spinach (add towards the end of the cooking time)

1. Preheat the oven to 200°C/180°C fan/Gas Mark 6.

2. Heat the oil in a large saucepan over a medium heat, then add the onions and peppers, stirring regularly until softened, about 10 minutes. Add the garlic, cumin, oregano, smoked paprika and chilli powder and cook until the aromas hit you, for a minute or so.

3. Add the chicken, tomatoes and pineapple (along with any additions) and increase the heat to bring to the boil, then reduce the heat to low and simmer for about 15–20 minutes until the chicken is cooked through (if using frozen chicken, it may need a little longer). Season with salt and pepper to taste.

4. Divide the mixture (leaving behind any excess liquid) amongst the tortilla wraps, roll the filled wraps and fold over the edges to seal, then split the enchiladas between two ovenproof casserole dishes. Drizzle over any remaining sauce, then sprinkle with Cheddar and bake in the oven for 15–20 minutes until bubbling and golden, then serve.

FREEZE:
Cool completely at the end of step 3, then portion up (you can wrap each enchilada separately) and wrap in foil, then pop into a resealable freezer bag and put into the freezer.

FREEZER TO TABLE:
Place the foil-wrapped enchiladas into an ovenproof dish. Cook in an oven preheated to 200°C/180°C fan/Gas Mark 6 for 30–45 minutes until piping hot through. Uncover for the final 5 minutes. Or defrost overnight in the fridge and halve the oven timings.

Butternut Squash & Sage Pasta Bake

SERVES 8–10 (4–6 FOR NOW AND 4–6 FOR LATER) • 10 MINUTES PREP • 45 MINUTES COOKING

Pasta bakes are a no-nonsense, anyone-can-do-it kind of dish. Usually a tomato base is the starting point, but I'd like you to meet this little number. Earthy, veg-heavy and truly divine. A great reason to stock up on those bags of frozen butternut squash (or freeze it yourself!).

1.5kg frozen butternut squash chunks, or 2 fresh butternut squash peeled and cut into 2.5cm chunks

500g pasta (penne, shells or farfalle are great)

2 large knobs of butter

2 onions, finely chopped

4 garlic cloves, finely chopped

1 bunch of sage, leaves picked and roughly chopped

1 litre vegetable stock

2 x 200ml pots crème fraîche

200g spinach, or 4–6 frozen spinach cubes

4 small packets (about 500g) mozzarella, pulled into strips

2 handfuls of grated Parmesan cheese

1. Preheat the oven to 220°C/200°C fan/Gas Mark 7.

2. Put the squash in a roasting tin and roast for 20–30 minutes, until tender, giving it a stir halfway through. Turn the oven down to 200°C/180°C fan/Gas Mark 6.

3. Cook the pasta according to the packet instructions.

4. Meanwhile, melt the butter in a large saucepan over a medium heat, then add the onions, stirring regularly, until golden and softened, about 10 minutes. Add the garlic and sage, stirring continuously, until the aroma hits you, for 20 seconds or so. Add the stock, crème fraîche, butternut squash plus any of the roasting juices, along with the spinach. Stir and allow to thicken.

5. Drain the pasta, then stir it into the saucepan with the butternut squash. Season with salt and pepper to taste, stir, then pour half into an ovenproof baking dish. Top with the mozzarella and Parmesan, bake in the oven for 15 minutes until golden and bubbling, then serve.

FREEZE:
Before pouring the pasta bake into the dish, line the dish with foil (with some overhang), or pour into individual ramekins. Top and bake as above; once it has cooled completely you can wrap the foil over the top and put the whole dish into the freezer to flash-freeze. Remove the frozen pasta bake from the dish to store it whole – put into a labelled resealable freezer bag or wrap well with more foil.

FREEZER TO TABLE:
Unwrap and place in a baking dish, cover with foil and bake for 45–60 minutes in an oven preheated to 200°C/180°C fan/Gas Mark 6 until piping hot through, uncovering for the final 5 minutes. Note that larger portions will take much longer to cook than smaller portions. Or defrost overnight in the fridge and halve the oven timings.

Vegetable Toad in the Hole

SERVES 8 (4 FOR NOW AND 4 FOR LATER) • 20 MINUTES PREP • 30 MINUTES COOKING

Most of us love a good toad in the hole but have you ever tried swapping the bangers for a rainbow of veg? It becomes a wonderfully earthy version of the original and works great with onion gravy too. Another winning way to finish off any root veg glut! As ever, do feel free to chop and change the quantity and type of veg to whatever you have in your kitchen.

4 eggs

240ml whole milk

200g plain flour

2 tsp baking powder

4 tsp wholegrain mustard

4 sprigs of rosemary, leaves chopped

2 tbsp olive oil, plus extra for drizzling

1kg root vegetables (carrots, beetroot, celeriac, parsnip, sweet potatoes etc.), peeled and cut into wedges

4 red onions, quartered (but root left intact)

2 peppers (ideally red, orange or yellow), deseeded and cut into chunks

2 courgettes, cut into chunks

300g butternut squash, frozen or fresh, cut into 3cm chunks

10 cherry tomatoes, halved

1. Preheat the oven to 220°C/200°C fan/Gas Mark 7.

2. Beat together the eggs, milk, flour, baking powder, mustard and rosemary leaves with the oil and a little salt and pepper. Let stand for 15 minutes.

3. Divide all the vegetables between two roasting tins, drizzle with oil and a little salt and pepper and bake for 20–25 minutes.

4. Increase the oven temperature to 240°C/220°C fan/ Gas Mark 9. Pour the batter mixture evenly into each tray of vegetables and return to the oven for 10 minutes, then reduce the heat to 220°C/200°C fan/ Gas Mark 7 and bake for a further 10–15 minutes until golden and puffed up.

❄ *Ice Kitchen Tip*
Any fresh leftover butternut squash can be blanched for a couple of minutes, cooled, flash-frozen on a tray, then put into a labelled resealable freezer bag.

 FREEZE:
Cool completely, portion up (I like preparing portions of two) and freeze flat in labelled resealable bags. To freeze the entire dish, line the tins with foil with overhang; once cool, wrap the foil over the top and put into the freezer. Once frozen solid, use the foil to lift out the toad in the hole, wrap with more foil and put into a labelled resealable freezer bag to return to the freezer.

 FREEZER TO TABLE:
Put into an ovenproof dish, cover with foil or a lid and bake in an oven preheated to 200°C/180°C fan/Gas Mark 6 for about 35–45 minutes until piping hot through. Note that larger portions will take much longer to cook than smaller portions.

Onion Gravy

SERVES 12 (4 FOR NOW AND 8 FOR LATER) · 5 MINUTES PREP · 35 MINUTES COOKING

This is a toad in the hole essential, but it's also great to have knocking around the freezer for things like sausages and mash and roasts.

3 large knobs of butter
9 large onions, thickly sliced
3 tbsp balsamic vinegar
3 tbsp flour
1.5 litres vegetable stock

1. Melt the butter in a large saucepan over a low heat. Add the onions with a large pinch of salt and the balsamic vinegar, stirring now and again, and cook until caramelised and sticky, about 50 minutes.

2. Stir in the flour, then add a couple of tablespoons of the stock, stirring vigorously to ensure there are no lumps in the flour mixture. Gradually add the rest of the stock and increase the heat to bring up to the boil. Cook for 5-10 minutes until thickened. Season with salt and pepper to taste.

FREEZER TO TABLE:
Empty into a lidded saucepan with an extra splash of water, then place over a medium heat until defrosted. Increase the heat and cook until piping hot through, stirring often, so that it doesn't stick or burn. Or defrost overnight in the fridge, before reheating on the hob.

FREEZE:
Cool completely, portion up and lie flat to freeze in labelled resealable bags. Once frozen 'file' upright.

Freezer Pizza

MAKES 8 SMALL PIZZAS • 5 MINUTES PREP • 15 MINUTES REST • 15 MINUTES COOKING

Long gone is the need for cardboard freezer pizza. Have your own, ready-to-go, *The Ice Kitchen* Method. I'm not just talking about dough, I mean a pizza with all the toppings, just the way you like it, ready to pop into the oven and on your table in 15 minutes. Pass the chilli flakes!

500g plain flour, plus extra for dusting

2 tsp fast-action dried yeast

2 tsp sea salt flakes

1 tsp sugar

2 tbsp extra-virgin olive oil

8 tbsp Swift Salvation Tomato Sauce (see page 115) or tomato passata

2 large balls of mozzarella, pulled into shreds

TOPPING IDEAS:

Chilli flakes

Parma ham

Fresh rocket

Smudges of 'nduja

Basil leaves

1. Preheat the oven to 220°C/200°C fan/Gas Mark 7 and line some baking trays with baking parchment.

2. Put all the dry ingredients into a large bowl and mix together. Make a well in the centre and pour in 300g warm water along with the extra-virgin olive oil. Stir to bring together into a wet dough. Dust your hands with flour and knead until smooth, about 5 minutes. Cover the bowl with a tea towel and leave to rest for about 15 minutes.

3. Divide the dough into 8 balls and roll each out on a floured surface as thin as you can. Transfer the pizza base to the lined baking trays and top as you like.

4. Pop into the oven for 8–10 minutes, until the cheese topping is bubbling and golden, and the pizza is cooked through.

❄ *Ice Kitchen Tip*
   You can also freeze the dough unrolled and defrost at room temperature (this will take approximately 2 hours). You'll need to roll, top and cook the pizzas as soon as the dough has defrosted, in an oven preheated to 220°C/200°C fan/Gas Mark 7 for about 10 minutes.

FREEZE:
Follow the recipe up to the end of step 3. Keep the pizza on the baking paper and double-wrap the whole pizza (baking paper too!) with foil, pop into a labelled resealable freezer bag, then put into the freezer.

FREEZER TO TABLE:
Remove the bag and foil (leave the baking paper underneath) and bake in an oven preheated to 220°C/200°C fan/Gas Mark 7 for 10–15 minutes until cooked through and golden and bubbling on top.

Carrot & Coriander Soup

SERVES 8–12 (4–6 FOR NOW AND 4–6 FOR LATER) • 10 MINUTES PREP • 30 MINUTES COOKING

Soup has always been a great way to use up a glut of veg (which is very much one of the key principles of *The Ice Kitchen* Method). This is a big favourite of mine as no matter what I cook during the week, I always seem to end up with a ridiculous amount of carrots and onions! Thank goodness I am obsessed with this soup … Change the spicing to give it a different flavour.

glug of oil

4 onions, roughly chopped

5 garlic cloves, roughly chopped

10 medium or large carrots (about 1–1.5kg), sliced

2 heaped tsp ground coriander

2–3 litres vegetable or chicken stock (depending on how much carrot you put in)

SWAP THE GROUND CORIANDER FOR:

— *generous pinch of chilli powder and 2 heaped tsp ground cumin*

— *2 heaped tsp smoked paprika and 2 heaped tsp dried thyme*

— *2 heaped tsp harissa paste*

1. Heat the oil in a large saucepan over a medium heat, then add the onions, garlic, carrots and ground coriander. Cook, stirring regularly, until softened, about 10 minutes or so. Add the stock, increase the heat to bring up to the boil, then reduce the heat to low and simmer with the lid on for about 20 minutes.

2. Blitz with a blender, then return to the heat to thicken a little. Season with salt and pepper to taste and serve.

➜ *Try with* finely chopped fresh coriander leaves and toasted seeds (pumpkin works well) sprinkled on top.

 FREEZE:
Cool completely, then portion up (I like preparing portions of two) and lay flat to freeze in labelled resealable freezer bags, until solid.

 FREEZER TO TABLE:
Put into a lidded saucepan with an extra splash of water, then cover and place over a low heat until defrosted. Increase the heat and cook until piping hot through. Or defrost overnight in the fridge, before reheating on the hob.

Minestrone

SERVES 8–12 (4–6 FOR NOW AND 4–6 FOR LATER) • 15 MINUTES PREP • 30 MINUTES COOKING

This complete meal is a fantastic and easy-peasy canvas for a host of ingredients that you may need to use. It's also a great way to get fussy eaters and kids chowing down all the good stuff. I often make this a green minestrone by changing up some of the ingredients (see below). It certainly does well in the freezer; like many freezer dishes it comes out tasting even richer in flavour.

3 onions, quartered

12 carrots, roughly chopped

12 celery sticks, roughly chopped

4 generous glugs of olive oil

4 garlic cloves, crushed

3 litres vegetable stock

2 x 400g tins plum tomatoes

2 x 400g tins cannellini beans, drained

250g pasta (if you go for spaghetti, linguine, or other long pasta, do break it into pieces)

2 large handfuls of green veg (chopped courgettes, spinach, frozen peas, broad beans, cabbage, cavolo nero)

SWAP THE TINNED TOMATOES FOR:

— *more green veg and a spoonful of pesto*

1. Use a food processor to blitz together the onions, carrots and celery until finely chopped (or you can do this by hand).

2. Heat the oil in a large saucepan over a medium heat, then add the chopped onion, carrot, celery and the garlic and cook, stirring regularly, until softened, about 10 minutes. Add the stock and tinned tomatoes, cover with a lid and reduce the heat to low. Simmer for 10 minutes.

3. Add the cannellini beans, pasta and veg, put the lid back on and simmer for another 10 minutes, just until the pasta is cooked. Season with salt and pepper to taste.

→ **Try with** a spoonful of pesto, grated Parmesan, cooked sausage meat, a drizzle of extra-virgin olive oil.

 FREEZE:
Cool completely, portion up (I like preparing portions of two) and lay flat to freeze in labelled resealable freezer bags until solid, then 'file' upright in your freezer.

 FREEZER TO TABLE:
Empty into a lidded saucepan with an extra splash of water, then cover and place over a medium heat until defrosted. Increase the heat and cook until piping hot through, stirring often so that it doesn't stick or burn. Or defrost overnight in the fridge, before reheating on the hob.

Spanish Seafood Stew

SERVES 8 (4 FOR NOW AND 4 FOR LATER) • 10 MINUTES PREP • 30 MINUTES COOKING

It can be easy to disregard bags of frozen seafood, but it is usually flash-frozen moments after it comes out of the ocean (compared to some of the 'fresh' fish you buy, which is often frozen then defrosted). It is so handy to keep around for ease of cooking and eating. One-pot heaven bursting with flavour, you could easily think you were on the sunny Spanish coast.

2 glugs of olive oil

2 onions, finely chopped

3 garlic cloves, finely chopped

2 tbsp smoked paprika

1 tsp cayenne (for an optional kick)

2 small glasses of dry white wine (about 300ml)

2 x 400g tins chopped tomatoes

6 large potatoes, peeled and cut into 1cm cubes

2 tbsp tomato purée

2 chorizo rings, skin removed and roughly chopped

2 handfuls of pitted black olives

2 x 400g tins chickpeas, drained

2 x 400g bags frozen mixed seafood

4 tbsp finely chopped parsley leaves

1. Heat the oil in a large saucepan over a medium heat, add the onions and cook, stirring regularly, until softened, about 5–10 minutes. Add the garlic and spices and stir continuously until the aroma hits, for 30 seconds or so.

2. Add the wine, allow it to sizzle, then add the chopped tomatoes, potatoes and tomato purée, season with salt and pepper and simmer with the lid on for about 15 minutes until the potato is cooked through.

3. Add the chorizo, olives and chickpeas and halve the mixture. Add one bag of seafood to the For Now portion. Reduce the heat to low, cover and simmer for 10–15 minutes until the seafood is just cooked through. Season with salt and pepper to taste, sprinkle over the parsley and serve.

→ **Try with** crusty bread, wedges of lemon and a drizzle of extra-virgin olive oil.

❄ *Ice Kitchen Tip*
Flash-freeze leftover olives on a covered tray and pop into a labelled freezer bag, for making tapenade.

 FREEZE:
Follow the recipe up to step 3, and leave out the seafood. Allow to cool completely, portion up (I like preparing portions of two) and lay flat to freeze in labelled resealable freezer bags until solid, then 'file' upright.

FREEZER TO TABLE:
Empty into a saucepan with a splash of water, cover and place over a low heat until defrosted. Increase the heat and cook until piping hot through, stirring often. Add the frozen seafood, reduce the heat and simmer for 10–15 minutes until the seafood is just cooked through.

North African Chicken Traybake

SERVES 8 (4 FOR NOW AND 4 FOR LATER) • 10 MINUTES PREP • 50 MINUTES COOKING

Traybakes are the epitome of easy cooking and they really are a great way to use up leftover ingredients lying around the kitchen. Best of all, they freeze well and taste even better once reheated, truly embodying the Ice Kitchen's amazing capabilities! This combination of heady spices and sharp-flavoured ingredients is one of my all-time favourites.

16 chicken pieces (a mix of bone-in skin-on thighs and drumsticks)

1 large bag of new or baby potatoes (about 1.5kg), halved

8 preserved lemons, quartered

300g jar pitted green olives, drained

2 large onions, cut lengthways into eighths

6 garlic cloves, unpeeled and smashed

2 tsp ground cumin

2 tsp ground coriander

500ml chicken stock

4 tbsp extra-virgin olive oil

SWAP THE PRESERVED LEMONS, GREEN OLIVES, CUMIN AND CORIANDER FOR:

— *2 packets of chorizo, sliced, 2 tbsp smoked paprika, some sprigs of thyme, 2 thickly sliced peppers, thick slices of red onion, a couple*

of handfuls of black olives
— *thick slices of red onion, 4 courgettes cut into chunks, 2 thickly sliced peppers, zest and juice of 2 lemons, sprigs of fresh oregano (or 1 heaped tsp dried oregano)*

1. Preheat the oven to 200°C/180°C fan/Gas Mark 6.

2. Put all the ingredients into a roasting tin in a single layer (use 2 tins if necessary), give everything a good stir to mix well, add a little salt and pepper, cover with foil and bake in the oven for 30 minutes.

3. Remove the foil, then cook for another 20–30 minutes until cooked through and juices run clear and serve.

❋ *Ice Kitchen Tip*
Bone-in meat can take longer to heat through, especially when cooked from frozen. To be safe, I usually would always defrost these fully in the fridge overnight before heating until piping hot through.

FREEZE:
Allow to cool completely, then portion up (I like preparing portions of two) and place into labelled resealable freezer bags. Lay flat to freeze, before 'filing' upright.

FREEZER TO TABLE:
Put in the fridge overnight; once defrosted, empty into a roasting tin, cover with foil and bake for 45–55 minutes until piping hot through. Pop under a hot grill for a couple of minutes to crisp up the skins.

Beef & Prune Tagine

SERVES 8–12 (4–6 FOR NOW AND 4–6 FOR LATER) • 10 MINUTES PREP • 3 HOURS 10 MINUTES COOKING

Tagines are great meals to keep lying around in your 'freezer file', tasting ever better a week or so later, particularly this melt-in-the-mouth beef and prune version. This low-maintenance dish is totally worth it for your future meals bank.

2 large glugs of olive oil

2 tbsp ras el hanout

2 tbsp ground cinnamon

2 tbsp ground cumin

1–1.5kg stewing steak, cut into chunks

2 onions, finely chopped

4 garlic cloves, finely chopped

2 x 400g tins chopped tomatoes

2 beef stock cubes, crumbled

2 large sweet potatoes, chopped into bite-size chunks

16 large pitted prunes (about 200g), roughly chopped

TRY ADDING:

— 1–2 x 400g tins drained chickpeas, or diced root veg

1. Preheat the oven to 120°C/100°C fan/Gas Mark ½.

2. Heat the oil in a large ovenproof casserole over a medium heat. Add the spices then add the beef, in batches if necessary, to brown and seal. Add the onions, lower the heat and cook, stirring regularly, until softened, about 10 minutes. Add the garlic and stir continuously until the aromas hit you, about 20 seconds.

3. Add the tomatoes and stock cubes, plus a tinful of water. Add salt and pepper, give it a stir, put the lid on, then put it into the oven for 1½ hours.

4. Increase the heat to 150°C/130°C fan/Gas Mark 2. Add the sweet potatoes and prunes (plus the chickpeas and root veg, if using), give everything a stir and return to the oven for another 1½ hours, or until the potatoes are cooked through and tender. Season with salt and pepper to taste, then serve.

→ **Try with** couscous cooked in stock and roasted root veg.

 FREEZE:
Cool completely, then portion up (I like preparing portions of two) and pour into labelled resealable freezer bags. Lay the tagine flat to freeze, then store upright in your freezer 'file'.

FREEZER TO TABLE:
Empty into a lidded saucepan and place over a low-medium heat, breaking it up as it defrosts; once fully defrosted, add a splash of water, increase the heat and cook, stirring often, until piping hot through. Or defrost overnight in the fridge, before reheating on the hob.

Beef Rendang

SERVES 8 (4 FOR NOW AND 4 FOR LATER) • 15 MINUTES PREP • 2 HOURS COOKING

I fell in love at my first ever bite of a rendang, eaten at my father-in-law's home in food-haven Singapore, so skilfully made by Santi (boy, can she cook!). It ticks ALL the boxes: spicy, sweet, sour and savoury. Most of the cooking is done in the oven so it isn't laborious at all. This dish should really have a kick to it, but if that's not your style, by all means go easy on the chilli.

8 tbsp peeled and roughly chopped ginger

8 garlic cloves, roughly chopped

4 sticks of lemongrass, bulbs discarded and sticks chopped

4–8 bird's-eye/Thai chillies (depending on how hot you like it!)

4 glugs of oil

4 onions, finely chopped

4 cinnamon sticks

1.5–2kg beef shin or braising steak, diced

4 x 400g tins coconut milk

4 tbsp tamarind paste

8 kaffir lime leaves

20 heaped tbsp (about 200g) desiccated coconut

1. Blitz the ginger, garlic, lemongrass and chillies in a food processor to form a paste.

2. Heat the oil in a large saucepan over a high heat, add the paste and chopped onion and fry, stirring often, until the aroma is released and the mixture darkens, about 5 minutes. Add the cinnamon sticks and stir for another minute.

3. Add the beef and stir to coat in the paste, then add the coconut milk, tamarind paste and lime leaves. Reduce the heat to the lowest heat and simmer (without the lid) for 1½–2 hours, stirring regularly, until the sauce is reduced and thick and the meat is falling apart.

4. Toast the desiccated coconut in a dry frying pan until golden brown, then blitz (in a food processor) to a coarse powder.

5. Stir in the coconut, then continue to cook for another 20 minutes without the lid. Remove the cinnamon sticks, season with salt and pepper to taste and serve.

→ **Try with** fragrant rice.

FREEZE:
Cool completely, then portion up (I like preparing portions of two) and put into labelled resealable freezer bags. Lay flat to freeze then 'file' upright.

FREEZER TO TABLE:
Empty into a lidded saucepan and place over a low-medium heat, breaking it up as it defrosts. Once fully defrosted, add a splash of water, increase the heat and cook, stirring often, until piping hot through. Or defrost overnight in the fridge, before reheating on the hob.

Chipotle Pulled Pork

SERVES 8–12 (4–6 FOR NOW AND 4–6 FOR LATER) • 5 MINUTES PREP, PLUS MARINATING • 5½–7½ HOURS COOKING

Pulled pork can do no wrong in my eyes – it is great stuffed into a burger bun, mixed with rice or used to fill tacos or fajitas. The prep is easy peasy and it's a 'shove in the oven and wait' wonder, so it makes sense to prepare a massive joint, shred it into portions, freeze and have pulled pork at your fingertips, ready in a snip of time, *The Ice Kitchen* Method!

8 tbsp chipotle paste

4 tbsp cider vinegar

2 tbsp tomato purée

2.5kg skinless and boneless pork shoulder, slashed a few times with a sharp knife

200g orange juice

2 tbsp honey

SWAP THE CHIPOTLE PASTE FOR:

— *Jerk Marinade (see page 126)*

1. Mix together 6 tablespoons of the chipotle paste with the cider vinegar and tomato purée. Massage into the pork and, if possible, leave to marinate in the fridge overnight.

2. When you are ready to cook the pork, preheat the oven to 150°C/130°C fan/Gas Mark 2.

3. Put the pork into a deep-sided roasting tin, pour in the orange juice and cover with a 'tent' of foil, ensuring that it is sealed at the edges of the dish but doesn't actually touch the pork. Bake in the oven for 5–7 hours until the meat is falling apart. Check to make sure it hasn't dried out, topping up with a little more orange juice if needed.

4. Increase the heat to 200°C/180°C fan/Gas Mark 6 and remove the foil. Brush with the honey and cook for another 30 minutes until crisp and sticky. Remove any fatty bits of meat, then use a fork to pull the pork apart. Mix through the remaining 2 tablespoons of chipotle paste, ensuring all the juices coat the pulled meat. Season with salt and pepper to taste and serve.

→ **Try with** tacos and pickled pink onions and guacamole, or with rice and beans or in burger buns.

 FREEZE:
Cool quickly and completely, then portion up (I like preparing portions of two) and put into labelled resealable freezer bags. Lay flat to freeze, then 'file' upright.

 FREEZER TO TABLE:
Empty into a lidded saucepan and place over a low-medium heat, breaking it up as it defrosts. Once fully defrosted, add a splash of water, increase the heat and cook, stirring often, until piping hot through. Or defrost overnight in the fridge, before reheating on the hob.

Meatloaf

SERVES 8 (4 FOR NOW AND 4 FOR LATER) • 15 MINUTES PREP • 45 MINUTES COOKING

Meatloaf really is a superfood that *I would do anything for* (sorry, I always think of *that* song when I eat this); it's a delicious, filling, cost-effective eat that is totally retro and totally fantastic. You can change the mince, or change the seasoning or spicing to create a completely different flavour.

1 large glug of oil

2 onions, finely chopped

3 garlic cloves, grated or finely chopped

4 sprigs of thyme, leaves finely chopped

2 sprigs of rosemary, leaves finely chopped

800g–1kg pork mince

2 heaped tbsp tomato purée

200g breadcrumbs

150–200g bacon lardons (depending on the packet size)

2 eggs, beaten

SWAP THE THYME AND ROSEMARY FOR:

— *2 tbsp ground cumin, 2 tbsp ground coriander and 1 tsp chilli powder*

— *2 tsp chipotle paste*

1. Preheat the oven to 200°C/180°C fan/Gas Mark 6 and line the base and sides of two 900g loaf tins with baking parchment.

2. Heat the oil in a small frying pan over a medium heat, add the onions and fry until softened, about 5–10 minutes. Add the garlic and the herbs and fry until the aroma hits you, for 20 seconds or so. Set aside to cool.

3. When cool, tip into a large bowl, with the remaining ingredients along with a little salt and pepper and use your hands to mix and squash the mixture together.

4. Pat the mixture into the loaf tins. Put the tins on a baking tray and bake for 40–50 minutes until cooked through.

5. Place the loaf tins under a hot grill for about 5 minutes until the top of the loaf is brown, then serve.

→ **Try with** creamy mashed potato, greens and gravy, or a rich tomato sauce.

FREEZE:
Cool completely. You can either freeze the meatloaf whole, or slice into individual portions, with baking parchment separating each slice. Wrap in foil and freeze in a labelled resealable freezer bag.

FREEZER TO TABLE:
Unwrap the whole meatloaf and put back into the loaf tin, then cover with foil. Bake in an oven preheated to 200°C/180°C fan/Gas Mark 6 for 1–1½ hours (if heating smaller portions, wrap them in foil – you may need to reduce the timings; after the first 30 minutes, check at 15-minute intervals) until piping hot through, removing the foil for the last 10 minutes of cooking. Or defrost overnight in the fridge and halve the oven timings.

Sticky Ribs

SERVES 8 (4 FOR NOW AND 4 FOR LATER) • 5 MINUTES PREP • 3 HOURS 10 MINUTES COOKING

Having sticky fingers from (wo)manhandling ribs is definitely one of my happy places. I don't often make these because when I want them I want them NOW!, so it's well worth making a double batch of them and keeping them in the freezer for when that moment strikes. It won't be immediate eating, but it's as close as you can get to it. Freeze the sauce too for extra dipping and slathering.

2 glugs of oil
2 garlic cloves, crushed
1 tsp fennel seeds, crushed
4 tbsp honey
1 small bottle of ketchup
    (about 300g)
4 tbsp whisky (optional)
4 tbsp soy sauce
4 tbsp Worcestershire sauce
4 tbsp soft dark brown sugar
2kg pork ribs

1. Preheat the oven to 160°C/140°C fan/Gas Mark 3. Heat the oil in a medium-sized saucepan over a medium heat and fry the garlic with the fennel seeds, stirring continuously until the aroma hits you, about 20 seconds or so. Add the honey, ketchup, whisky (if using), soy sauce, Worcestershire sauce and brown sugar. Bring to the boil, then reduce the heat and simmer for 5–10 minutes until thickened. Season with salt and pepper to taste.

2. Put the ribs in a roasting tin and glaze generously with the sauce. Cover the tin with a 'tent' of foil, ensuring that the foil doesn't touch the ribs, and bake for 2 hours.

3. Remove the foil and re-glaze the ribs, then increase the heat to 200°C/180°C fan/Gas Mark 6 and bake uncovered for 30 minutes. Turn the ribs over, re-glaze and bake for a further 30 minutes. Glaze one more time and put under the grill for a couple of minutes and serve.

→ **Try with** extra sauce, corn on the cob, fries, coleslaw.

FREEZER TO TABLE:
Put the ribs into a roasting tin, glaze with extra sauce (see below) and cover with foil. Bake in an oven preheated to 200°C/180°C fan/Gas Mark 6 for 30–45 minutes until piping hot through. Or defrost overnight in the fridge and halve the oven timings. Defrost the sauce in the microwave, overnight in the fridge or on the hob in a lidded saucepan over a low-medium heat, breaking it up as it defrosts; once fully defrosted add a splash of water, increase the heat and cook, stirring often, until piping hot through.

FREEZE:
Cool completely, then portion up and place into labelled resealable freezer bags. Lay flat to freeze. The leftover sauce should be cooled completely, then frozen flat in a labelled freezer bag, before being 'filed' upright.

Ratatouille

SERVES 8–12 (4–6 FOR NOW AND 4–6 FOR LATER) • 10 MINUTES PREP • 45 MINUTES COOKING

A glut-buster for all your Mediterranean vegetables. There is something wonderfully comforting about a ratatouille, regardless of the time of year. Of course, if you have more of one ingredient than the other, tailor the recipe so that it works for you and your produce.

3 large glugs of olive oil

2 aubergines, thickly sliced

4 courgettes, thickly sliced

2 onions, thinly sliced

2 peppers, deseeded and cut into bite-size pieces

5 garlic cloves, crushed

few sprigs of thyme (or 2 tsp dried thyme)

2 x 400g tins chopped or plum tomatoes

4–6 tomatoes, chopped

2 tbsp red wine vinegar

large bunch of basil

1 tsp sugar

1. Heat a large glug of oil in a large saucepan over a low heat, add the aubergines and courgettes and cook, stirring regularly, until softened, about 5 minutes. Remove with a slotted spoon and set aside.

2. Add another glug of olive oil, increase the heat to medium and add the onions and peppers, stirring regularly until softened, about 5–10 minutes. Add the garlic and thyme, stirring continuously, until the aromas hit you, about 30 seconds or so. Add the softened aubergine and courgette, along with the tinned tomatoes, chopped tomatoes, red wine vinegar, basil and sugar.

3. Reduce the heat to low and simmer for about 30 minutes until thick and glossy. Season with salt and pepper to taste and serve.

→ **Try with** hunks of warm crusty bread, a drizzle of extra-virgin olive oil, fresh basil leaves, chilli flakes if you fancy a little kick.

FREEZE:
Allow to cool completely, then portion up (I like preparing portions of two) and lay flat to freeze in labelled resealable freezer bags, until solid.

FREEZER TO TABLE:
Empty into a lidded saucepan with an extra splash of water, then place over a low heat until defrosted. Increase the heat and cook until piping hot through, stirring often, so that it doesn't stick or burn. Or defrost overnight in the fridge, before reheating on the hob.

Cheat's Jamaican Beef Patties

MAKES 8 LARGE OR 16 SMALL PATTIES · 20 MINUTES PREP · 45 MINUTES COOKING

Of course I HAD to include some proper Caribbean flavours in this book; these patties were an obvious front-runner. They are the definition of irresistible and a regular go-to in my household. These so remind me of my friend, Milli Taylor, who makes a mean version of my original patties (and gets me drooling when I see them on her mouth-watering Instagram feed). Making pastry from scratch can be a bit of a faff, so I've provided a clever cheat using shop-bought shortcrust pastry. I always go for beef or goat patties, but it is very easy to vary the fillings. If you plan to make lots of these to freeze, make sure that you use previously unfrozen pastry.

FOR THE PASTRY:

2 x 500g blocks shortcrust pastry (previously unfrozen)
2 tsp ground turmeric
2 tsp Madras curry powder
1 beaten egg

FOR THE FILLING:

2 glugs of oil
2 onions, finely diced
6 large garlic cloves, crushed
4 tsp curry powder
5 tbsp chopped chives
3 tbsp chopped thyme leaves
400–500g lean beef mince
200ml beef stock
2 tsp molasses sugar
2 tsp hot pepper sauce (optional, if you like it spicy)
2 slices of bread, torn into tiny pieces

1. Preheat the oven to 220°C/200°C fan/Gas Mark 7 and line a baking tray with baking parchment.

2. Heat the oil in a deep saucepan over a medium heat, add the onion and a little pinch of salt and cook, stirring regularly until softened, about 5–10 minutes.

3. Add the garlic, curry powder and herbs and stir continuously until the aromas hit you, about 30 seconds or so. Add the beef mince, breaking it up with a wooden spoon, and allow it to brown all over, then add the stock, sugar and hot pepper sauce. Increase the heat, bring up to the boil, then reduce the heat to low, cover the pan with a lid and let the mixture simmer for about 10 minutes.

4. Add the bread, then let the mixture continue to simmer for a further 10 minutes until thickened and rich. Remove the pan from the heat, season with salt and pepper to taste and leave to cool.

DROP THE TURMERIC EGG
WASH AND SWAP THE BEEF
FILLING FOR:

— *chicken, chorizo, potato,
  thyme and smoked paprika*
— *ham, pea and ricotta*
— *potato cheese and onion*

5. Roll the pastry out to a thickness of 5mm. Cut out
   8 circles about 18cm in diameter (use a side plate as a
   guide), or half that size if you want mini patties. Spoon
   the cooled filling on to one half of each pastry circle,
   leaving space at the edge to allow for sealing the
   pastry. Using your fingertip and a little water, wet the
   edges of the pastry and fold the non-filled half of the
   pastry over the filled half and use a fork to press down
   the edge.

6. Mix the turmeric and curry powder with the beaten
   egg, then generously brush half the filled patties with
   the mixture.

7. Bake in the oven for 20–25 minutes until golden, then
   serve.

→ *Try with* a simple green salad.

FREEZE:
Freeze the filled patties before glazing and
baking (at the end of step 5). Place them on
a tray lined with baking parchment, cover
and put into the freezer to flash-freeze. Once
frozen, transfer to a resealable freezer bag.

FREEZER TO TABLE:
Put the unwrapped patties on a baking
sheet lined with baking parchment, brush
with the turmeric curry powder egg wash
and bake in an oven preheated to 200°C/180°C
fan/Gas Mark 6 for 40–50 minutes until golden
and piping hot through.

Katsu Curry

SERVES 4 FOR NOW AND 4 FOR LATER • 15 MINUTES PREP • 20 MINUTES COOKING

I was obsessed with the katsu curry at Wagamamas … so one day I made my own and I have never looked back. I literally drink this sauce, so it's no wonder I always have some portioned up and ready to go in my freezer. It is so versatile and works as well with crumbed aubergine or breaded white fish as it does with the chicken.

FOR THE CHICKEN

4 eggs, beaten

10 tbsp flour, mixed with a little salt and pepper

12 heaped tbsp panko breadcrumbs

8 skinless chicken breasts

vegetable oil, for drizzling

FOR THE CURRY SAUCE

glug of oil

2 large onions, roughly chopped

4 large carrots, thinly sliced

6 large garlic cloves, roughly chopped

4 heaped tbsp mild curry powder

1 litre chicken or vegetable stock

2 tbsp honey

2 tbsp soy sauce

2 tbsp peanut butter

SWAP THE CHICKEN FOR:
— *crumbed aubergine (see page 152)*
— *fish goujons (see Crumbing, opposite)*

1. Preheat the oven to 200°C/180°C fan/Gas Mark 6 and lightly grease a baking tray. Put the beaten eggs, seasoned flour and breadcrumbs in separate shallow bowls.

2. For the chicken, coat the chicken breast in the flour, then the egg and then the breadcrumbs and set aside on a tray (use one hand for the dry dunking and the other for the wet dunking to avoid claggy fingers). Repeat with the remaining chicken breasts, drizzle them with a little vegetable oil, then arrange on the baking tray and bake in the oven for about 25 minutes until cooked through and golden, turning halfway.

3. Meanwhile, make the sauce. Heat the oil in a large saucepan over a medium heat and add the onions and carrots, stirring regularly until softened, about 5–10 minutes. Then add the garlic and curry powder and stir continuously until the aromas are released, for about 20 seconds or so.

4. Add the stock, increase the heat and bring up to the boil, then reduce the heat to low and simmer for 20 minutes, stirring now and again. Remove from the heat and use a hand-held blender to carefully blitz until the sauce is smooth (or pour into a blender and blitz until smooth).

5. Return to the heat, add the honey, soy sauce and peanut butter and simmer over a low heat for another 5 minutes until the sauce has thickened. Season with salt and pepper to taste.

6. Remove the baked chicken from the oven and slice, then drizzle the katsu sauce over and serve.

FREEZE:
To freeze the sauce: cool completely, then portion up (I like preparing portions of two) and place into labelled resealable freezer bags. Lay flat to freeze.

To freeze the chicken: place the breaded, uncooked chicken on a baking sheet, cover and flash-freeze. Once frozen, place in a labelled resealable freezer bag.

FREEZER TO TABLE:
Put the frozen katsu curry sauce into a lidded saucepan and place over a low-medium heat, breaking it up as it defrosts;

once fully defrosted, add a splash of water, increase the heat and cook, stirring often, until piping hot through. Or defrost in the microwave in a covered microwaveable dish; use the defrost setting in short bursts, breaking up and stirring as necessary, then heat on the high setting, in short bursts, stirring often, until piping hot through. Or defrost overnight in the fridge, before reheating on the hob.

Put the frozen breaded chicken breasts on to a greased, hot baking tray, drizzle with a little oil and bake in an oven preheated to 200°C/180°C fan/Gas Mark 6 for 20–25 minutes, turning over halfway through cooking, until golden and cooked through.

Crumbing

It is most definitely worth keeping a freezer stashed with chicken or fish goujons. The best way to crumb is by creating a 'crumbing station': one bowl of seasoned flour, one bowl with the beaten egg, and one bowl with panko breadcrumbs. Dip your goujon into the flour, then the egg, then the breadcrumbs and set aside on a baking tray. (It will be messy but to avoid carnage use one hand for the flour and breadcrumbs and the other for the egg.)

Breadcrumbs Use a food processor to whizz up stale bread to make your breadcrumbs, or buy panko breadcrumbs for a crispier crumb.

Add flavour For roughly every 50g of breadcrumbs add 1 tablespoon of the following: chilli powder, finely chopped herbs (dill or parsley works well with fish), cayenne powder, Cajun spices. Or add grated Parmesan and the zest of a lemon for a different flavour kick.

Chicken The general rule for chicken is to freeze the crumbed, uncooked chicken on a covered baking tray, to flash-freeze. When frozen, put them into a resealable freezer bag. To cook from frozen, put on to a baking sheet, drizzle lightly with oil then cook for 25–30 minutes (of course this also depends on the size of goujon) in an oven preheated to 200°C/180°C fan/Gas Mark 6, turning halfway, until golden and piping hot.

Fish The general rule for fish is to flash-freeze the crumbed, uncooked fish on a covered baking tray. When frozen, put them into a resealable freezer bag. To cook from frozen, put on to a baking sheet, drizzle lightly with oil and bake in an oven preheated to 200°C/180°C fan/Gas Mark 6 for 15–25 minutes (of course this also depends on the size of the goujon). Turn halfway through cooking, until golden and piping hot and cooked through.

Salvation Suppers

Salvation sounds a bit extreme, but actually this collection of recipes below have been just that for me, when I've got home from a hectic day, the little Chunk is screaming his head off and my big boy is reciting on repeat 'What's for dinner? What's for dinner? What's for dinner?' Pure wizardry …

One Base Many Ways

One base (to rule them all) and ... that can be switched up into so many meals. That is the gist of this group of very magic recipes. Really quite a clever way to use the freezer to its max, I think.

MIXED VEG

Frozen veg, whether you slice, dice and bag your own or stock up on the shop-bought convenience bags, needn't be just an afterthought side dish, it is fantastic to have at your fingertips! Not only does it retain the nutrients, making it often more nutritious than the veg just sitting in your fridge drawer for days, but it is so handy to have an array of colourful ingredients chopped and ready to go to make delicious meals. You'll find it much easier to hit your five-(or ten) a-day target! Most supermarket mixed veg contain a variation on carrot, peas, peppers, sweetcorn – make your own by chopping up these vegetables, or your own blend, into small ½–1cm cubes (removing any seeds and stems), flash-freezing on a covered tray, then transferring to a labelled resealable freezer bag to freeze.

Easiest Veg Stir-fry

SERVES 4 FOR NOW • 10 MINUTES PREP • 15 MINUTES COOKING

You can't beat a veggie-packed stir-fry midweek.

2 generous glugs of sesame oil

2 spring onions, finely chopped

2 garlic cloves, finely chopped

2.5cm piece of fresh ginger, peeled and finely chopped

2 large handfuls of frozen mixed veg (like peas, sweetcorn, carrot, broccoli, peppers, spinach)

4 tbsp hoisin sauce

4 tbsp soy sauce

300–500g noodles, cooked as per packet instructions

TRY ADDING:
— fresh or frozen strips of raw or pre-cooked chicken at step 1, ensuring that any raw chicken is cooked through before adding the veg

1. Heat the sesame oil in a wok over a high heat, then add the spring onions, garlic and ginger and fry, stirring constantly, until the aroma hits you, about 30 seconds.

2. Add the vegetables and fry, stirring and moving them around constantly for about 5–10 minutes until they are just cooked with a little crunch. Stir in the hoisin and soy sauces. Toss the cooked noodles through the saucy veg and season with salt and pepper to taste and serve.

→ **Try with** thinly sliced red chilli and 1 tbsp toasted sesame seeds.

Mixed Veg
Cheat's Vegetable Samosas

MAKES 12 FOR NOW · 20 MINUTES PREP · 45 MINUTES COOKING

A little more time is needed here, but it's mostly time spent in the oven. The filo folding bit is really very simple and I treat it as a moment of meditation during a busy week!

2 large glugs of oil

1 onion, finely chopped

2 garlic cloves, finely chopped

2 tsp garam masala

½ tsp ground turmeric

pinch of chilli powder

1 small potato (sweet or white), finely diced and boiled until tender

2 handfuls of frozen mixed small veg (peas, carrots, sweetcorn and peppers work really well)

1 tbsp chopped coriander leaves

1 packet of filo pastry (if frozen, leave to defrost)

melted butter, for brushing

1 tbsp sesame seeds

1. Preheat the oven to 200°C/180°C fan/Gas Mark 6 and line a baking tray with baking parchment.

2. Heat the oil in a large frying pan over a medium heat, then add the onion, stirring until softened, about 5–10 minutes. Add the garlic and spices and stir continuously until the aroma hits you, about 20 seconds, then add the potato and frozen veg. Cook for about 10 minutes until the veg is heated through. Season with salt and pepper, stir in the coriander leaves and set aside to cool.

3. Unroll the filo pastry and peel off one sheet of filo, covering the remaining sheets with cling film so that they don't dry out. Lay the filo on your work surface and brush with butter. Fold in one third of the pastry towards the centre, brush with butter again, then fold the other third into the centre, so you end up with one long strip, made up of three layers.

4. Brush the strip with melted butter. Place a heaped teaspoon of filling off centre, about 2.5cm from the end of the pastry strip that is nearest you. Fold over one of the corners to cover the filling to make a triangle shape. Then fold the filling over, keeping the triangle shape. Continue folding, making sure that all points are tucked in. Brush with butter and sprinkle over a few sesame seeds. Continue until you have used up all your filling. Put the samosas on to the baking sheet and bake for 20–25 minutes, turning halfway through, until golden and crisp, then serve.

→ **Try with** mango chutney.

Mixed Veg
Vegetable Pot Pies

SERVES 4 FOR NOW • 15 MINUTES PREP • 35 MINUTES COOKING

Just uttering the words 'pot pie' fill me with deep comfort. This in-a-jiff version is bliss.

2 knobs of butter

1 onions, finely chopped

2 garlic cloves, finely chopped

2 sprigs of thyme, leaves finely chopped

3 tbsp flour, plus extra for dusting

5 tbsp whole milk

250ml vegetable stock

½ tsp grated nutmeg

1 large sweet potatoes, cut into small cubes

4 handfuls of frozen mixed veg (a large range is great here)

2 tbsp finely chopped parsley leaves

1 x ready-rolled sheet of puff pastry (or a block of puff pastry rolled out to a thickness of 5mm), defrosted if frozen

1 egg yolk, beaten with 1 tbsp milk

1. Preheat the oven to 220°C/200°C fan/Gas Mark 7.

2. Melt the butter in a large saucepan over a medium heat, then add the onions, stirring regularly until softened, about 10 minutes. Add the garlic and thyme, stirring continuously, until the aroma hits you, for 20 seconds or so. Add the flour and mix until well combined, then add the milk and stock, continually stirring until thickened and smooth.

3. Add the nutmeg, then the sweet potato and frozen veg. Put the lid on and cook until the vegetables are warm and the sweet potato is cooked through. Stir in the parsley leaves and season with salt and pepper to taste. Transfer the veg to four individual ramekins or pour into a deep ovenproof dish.

4. Unroll the pastry on to a floured surface. Brush the edge of the pie dish with water and stick the pastry on top or cut the pastry into 4 equal pieces and position on top of the individual ramekins. Use a knife to pierce a 1cm vent in the centre of the lids and brush with the egg and milk glaze. Put on to a baking tray and bake in the oven for 25–30 minutes until the pastry has puffed up and is golden brown, then serve.

MINCE

Now this is the way to true weeknight ease. A simple base to make in bulk that can be quickly transformed into a host of delicious flavours for a homemade saviour during those busier days. Because it is packed with veg, it also bulks out the mince, making it not only a cost-effective choice, but also one that provides you with more of your five-a-day, while reducing the amount of meat you are eating (without you noticing). Note: If you are using the base from just cooked (unfrozen), add it at the stage in the recipe where it says, 'once defrosted'.

Mince Base

MAKES 4 MEALS OF YOUR CHOICE TO SERVE 4 • 10 MINUTES PREP • 20 MINUTES COOKING

2 large glugs of oil

2 large onions, finely chopped

2 large carrots, finely diced

1 celery stick, finely chopped

1 large green pepper, deseeded and finely chopped

4 garlic cloves, finely chopped

handful of mushrooms, torn or finely chopped

1.5kg beef, pork, lamb, turkey, vegetarian or vegan mince, or a mix

1. Heat the oil in a large frying pan over a medium heat, then add the onions, carrots, celery and pepper, stirring regularly until softened, about 10 minutes. Add the garlic and stir continuously until the aroma hits you, about 20 seconds or so. Add the mushrooms and stir until wilted, then finally add the beef and brown all over, stirring often. Season with salt and pepper to taste.

❊ *Ice Kitchen Tip*
Any leftover mushrooms can be flash-frozen on a covered tray then transferred to a labelled resealable freezer bag.

 FREEZE:
Leave to cool then portion up into servings of 4 (or more – sometimes I like to portion up into 8 servings of 2, then halve the quantities in the below recipes). Put into labelled resealable freezer bags to freeze.

Mince
Midweek Bolognese

SERVES 4 · 5 MINUTES PREP · 20-30 MINUTES COOKING

One of the ultimate comfort meals, here is a quick, but nonetheless satisfying version. This also makes a great base for a lasagne.

2 large glugs of olive oil

1 large garlic clove, smashed

1 heaped tsp dried oregano

400g tin chopped tomatoes

enough milk to fill ¼ of the empty tomato tin

1 stock cube

1 x 4-serving portion of frozen mince base

extra veg, such as torn mushrooms, diced carrots or frozen peas

1 tbsp finely chopped parsley leaves

1. Heat the oil in a large saucepan over a medium heat, then add the garlic and oregano, stirring continuously until the aromas hit you, about 30 seconds or so. Add the tinned tomatoes and a tinful of water, along with the milk, and crumble in the stock cube. Add the frozen mince base and cook over a medium-low heat with the lid on, breaking up the mince as it defrosts.

2. Once defrosted (if using unfrozen mince base, add it now), increase the heat, remove the lid and add any extra veg you wish. Cook, stirring often so that it doesn't catch, until the mince is cooked and piping hot through and the sauce has thickened, about 15 minutes. Remove the garlic clove, season with salt and pepper to taste, then stir through the parsley, and serve.

→ *Try with* cooked spaghetti and grated Parmesan or Cheddar cheese.

❋ *Ice Kitchen Tip*
Any leftover stock can be portioned and frozen in ice-cube trays (covered) before being put into labelled resealable freezer bags.

Mince
Midweek Chilli

SERVES 4 · 10 MINUTES PREP · 20–30 MINUTES COOKING

A pot of veg-charged chilli is sometimes exactly what is needed midweek: comfort, goodness and spice to dust off those cobwebs and push you through to the weekend!

2 large glugs of olive oil

1 large garlic clove, smashed

1½ tsp ground cumin

1½ tsp ground coriander

½–1 tsp chilli powder (depending on how hot you like it)

400g tin chopped tomatoes

1 stock cube

1 x 4-serving portion of frozen mince base

400g tin kidney beans, drained

extra veg, such as torn mushrooms, diced carrots or sweetcorn

1½ tbsp finely chopped coriander leaves

1. Heat the oil in a large saucepan over a medium heat, then add the garlic and spices, stirring continuously until the aromas hit you, about 30 seconds or so. Add the tinned tomatoes, along with a tinful of water, and crumble in the stock cube. Add the frozen mince base, cover and cook over a medium-low heat with the lid on, breaking up the mince as it defrosts.

2. Once defrosted (if using unfrozen mince base, add it now), increase the heat, remove the lid and cook, adding the kidney beans and any extra veg you wish. Cook, stirring often so that it doesn't catch, until the mince is cooked and piping hot through and the sauce has thickened, about 15 minutes. Remove the garlic and season with salt and pepper to taste. Stir through the coriander and serve.

→ **Try with** cooked rice, tortilla chips or sweet potato wedges and diced avocado.

❄ *Ice Kitchen Tip*
Any leftover soft herbs, like coriander, can be chopped, portioned into ice-cube trays (covered) before being put into labelled resealable freezer bags, to use in cooking.

Mince
Midweek Cottage Pie

SERVES 4 • 5 MINUTES PREP • 35 MINUTES COOKING

Another simple midweek magic comfort number, you can throw this together in two shakes of a lamb's (or should I say cow's) tail.

4 medium potatoes, peeled and cut into large chunks

large knob of butter

handful of grated Cheddar cheese, plus extra for sprinkling

splash of milk

2 large glugs of olive oil

1 large garlic clove, smashed

3 sprigs of fresh thyme (or 1½ tsp dried thyme)

1 heaped tbsp plain flour

1 stock cube

2 tbsp Worcestershire sauce

1 tbsp brown sauce

1 x 4-serving portion of frozen mince base

large handful of extra veg, such as torn mushrooms, diced carrots or frozen peas

1. Preheat the oven to 220°C/200°C fan/Gas Mark 7.

2. Boil the potatoes in a large saucepan of salted water until soft. Drain and mash well with the butter, Cheddar and milk. Season with salt and pepper to taste and set aside.

3. Heat the oil in a large saucepan over a medium heat, then add the garlic and thyme, stirring continuously until the aromas hit you, about 30 seconds or so. Stir in the flour until well combined then crumble in the stock cube, along with 250g water, stirring continuously to avoid any lumps. Add the Worcestershire and brown sauce and the frozen mince base and cook over a medium-low heat with the lid on, breaking up the mince as it defrosts.

4. Once defrosted (if using unfrozen mince base, add it now), increase the heat, remove the lid and add any extra veg you wish. Cook, stirring often so that it doesn't catch, until the mince is cooked and piping hot through. Remove the garlic and thyme sprigs, then season with salt and pepper to taste. Cook for a few more minutes to thicken into a glossy, rich sauce.

5. Pour the mince into a deep baking dish. Spoon and smooth over the mashed potato topping and sprinkle over the extra cheese. Bake in the oven for 15–20 minutes until golden on top, then serve.

Mince
Midweek Tacos

SERVES 4 • 5 MINUTES PREP • 20–30 MINUTES COOKING

This really couldn't be any easier to throw together. Prepare an array of toppings and let everyone pile in for a retro, hard-shell taco, DIY-style feast.

1 large glug of olive oil
1 large garlic clove, smashed
1½ tbsp ground cumin
1½ tbsp smoked paprika
1 tbsp dried oregano
1 tsp chilli powder
1 x 4-serving portion of frozen mince base

TO SERVE:
1 packet of crunchy taco shells
1 chopped iceberg lettuce
large handful of grated Cheddar cheese
3 diced vine tomatoes
smashed avocado
finely chopped red chillies
chopped coriander leaves

1. Remove the frozen mince base from the freezer and set aside at room temperature while you start the recipe.

2. Heat the oil a large saucepan over a medium heat and add the garlic and spices, stirring continuously until the aromas hit you, about 30 seconds or so. Add the mince base, along with a splash of water, and cook over a medium-low heat, breaking it up as it defrosts.

3. Once defrosted (if using unfrozen mince base, add it now), increase the heat and cook, stirring often, until the mince is piping hot and cooked through. Remove the garlic and season with salt and pepper to taste (the mixture should be dry), and serve with the taco shells, extra fillings and toppings.

CHICKEN

Why you wouldn't keep a bag of chicken in small strips in your freezer is beyond me. Such a clever hack can change your midweek meal from 'meh' to 'yeah' in minutes. The small strip sizing is key as it ensures that the chicken cooks quickly and you can use exactly the amount that you need – how convenient is that! Here are a few of our household's favourite go-to recipes. Remember, if you use frozen strips that are cooked, you won't be able to refreeze the finished dish.

Chicken Strips Base

5 MINUTES PREP

skinless and boneless
    chicken breasts, thighs, or
    cooked chicken

1. Use kitchen scissors to cut the chicken into 2cm-thick strips, then flash-freeze on a covered tray.

❋ *Ice Kitchen Tip*
    If you have any leftover roast chicken, strip it, flash-freeze it and throw it into labelled resealable freezer bags to be used in a range of delicious dishes.

 FREEZE:
Once frozen, throw into a resealable freezer bag and return to the freezer; simply grab handfuls as and when needed.

Chicken

Chicken & Mushroom Stroganoff

SERVES 4 FOR NOW · 10 MINUTES PREP · 30 MINUTES COOKING

Retro and classic at the same time. A hit with kids and adults alike and so comforting.

1 large glug of oil

1 onion, roughly chopped

3 large garlic cloves, grated

4 sprigs of thyme

1 tbsp smoked paprika

500g mushrooms, roughly chopped

1 vegetable stock cubes, crumbled

2–3 large handfuls of frozen raw chicken strips

75ml soured cream (or crème fraîche)

1 tbsp finely chopped parsley leaves

1. Heat the oil in a large saucepan over a low heat, and add the onions, stirring regularly until softened, about 5 minutes. Add the garlic, thyme and paprika and stir continuously until the aromas hit you, about 20 seconds or so.

2. Add the mushrooms, vegetable stock, 800ml just-boiled water and the chicken. Increase the heat to bring to the boil, then reduce the heat to low and cook for 20 minutes, stirring often, until the chicken is piping hot or cooked through. Stir in the soured cream or crème fraîche and parsley, bring the heat back up and cook for a further 5–10 minutes until thick and saucy, then serve.

→ *Try with* white rice, or mashed potato.

❄ *Ice Kitchen Tip*
Any leftover soft herbs like parsley can be chopped, portioned and frozen in ice-cube trays (covered) before being put into labelled resealable freezer bags, to be used in cooking.

Chicken
Mexican Shredded Chicken Soup

SERVES 4 FOR NOW · 15 MINUTES PREP · 20 MINUTES COOKING

This light and refreshing chicken soup has such incredible flavours I can't understand why it isn't better known. You can even add cooked rice to it if you fancy bulking it up.

2 tbsp oil

1 onion, finely chopped

3 garlic cloves, finely chopped

1 tsp ground cumin

1 dried ancho chilli, finely chopped (I find using scissors to cut it up much easier!)

400g tin plum tomatoes

1 litre chicken stock

400g tin black beans, drained

165g tin sweetcorn, drained

$1/2$ tsp sugar

2–3 large handfuls of frozen raw chicken strips

zest and juice of 2 limes

1. Heat the oil in a large saucepan over a medium heat, then add the onions, stirring regularly until softened, about 5–10 minutes. Add the garlic, cumin and chilli, stirring continuously, until the aromas hit you, for 20 seconds or so.

2. Add the remaining ingredients, except for the lime zest and juice. Increase the heat to bring up to the boil, then reduce the heat to low and simmer for 15–20 minutes until the chicken is piping hot or cooked through.

3. Stir in the lime zest and juice and season with salt and pepper to taste. You can shred the chicken at this stage, if you like, then serve.

→ **Try with** tortilla chips, guacamole and soured cream.

Ice Kitchen Twists with Frozen Chicken Strips

So many of the vegetarian recipes in *The Ice Kitchen* (and indeed the Ice Kitchen ethos itself!) lend themselves to an easy chop and change by the simple addition of our clever frozen chicken strips. Here are a few of my favourites that work perfectly with the addition of our frozen cluck-clucks. Feel free to experiment by adding them to your own favourite Ice Kitchen recipes too!

Chicken & Pineapple Fried Coconut Rice

Follow the recipe for Pineapple Fried Coconut Rice on page 46, adding the frozen chicken strips at step 3.

Chicken Pot Pie

Follow the recipe for Vegetable Pot Pies (see page 96), adding the frozen chicken strips at step 2.

Coconut Chicken Curry

Defrost a portion of Swift Salvation Coconut Curry Sauce (see page 116) in a saucepan. Add the frozen chicken strips, along with some veg (such as small cubes of sweet potato, a handful of spinach and a tin of drained chickpeas). Increase the heat and bring to the boil, then reduce the heat to low and simmer, stirring often, until the chicken and veg are cooked through and tender. Season with salt and pepper to taste and eat with rice, or Spiced Flatbreads (see page 135).

Feasts-in-foil

This is a clever way to create a complete meal parcel for one that you can have from freezer to table in a jiffy. It's also a great way to stock up those icy drawers. I would definitely recommend putting an hour aside on a weekend to get batch-cooking these parcels of perfection. What is magical about this bank of meals is that if you have built up a good store of them, everyone in the family can eat exactly what they want, without any real hassle at all! Other than having cooked rice at the ready, the prep is so simple and can be a great way to use odds and ends lying around at the bottom of the fridge. These are flavour combinations that I find work beautifully, but make this up just the way you want. A new, fresh approach to ready meals right here!

Sriracha Chicken & Broccoli

250g rice (or use 16 heaped tbsp pre-cooked rice)

4 small skinless and boneless chicken breasts or 8 thighs, diced

4 small handfuls of frozen peas

1 small head of broccoli, cut into florets

4 generous drizzles of sesame oil

4 generous dashes of soy sauce

2 garlic cloves, finely chopped (or use a pinch of garlic powder)

a few generous squirts of sriracha (as spicy as you like it)

4 squeezes of lime juice

Mexican Beef

250g rice (or use 16 heaped tbsp pre-cooked rice)

500g beef mince

2 garlic cloves, grated

2 tomatoes, diced

4 tsp ground cumin

4 tsp chipotle paste (or use 2 tsp ground cumin and 2 tsp chilli powder)

8 tbsp black beans

1 small onion, finely chopped

Spanish Chorizo

250g rice (or use 16 heaped tbsp pre-cooked rice)

1 chorizo ring, cut into 5mm slices

1 small jar or tin of pitted black olives, sliced

pinch of smoked paprika

1 pepper, chopped

4 sprigs of thyme

generous glug of olive oil

Japanese Salmon

250g rice (or use 16 heaped tbsp pre-cooked rice)

4 small salmon fillets (or use cod)

4 spring onions, thinly sliced

2 garlic cloves, finely chopped

1 tsp grated fresh ginger

4 tbsp white miso paste

2 tsp brown sugar

12 generous splashes of mirin

generous glug of sesame oil

1 small pack of asparagus tips, chopped

1. Cook the rice in a saucepan of boiling salted water according to the packet instructions. Drain and set aside to cool slightly in a large bowl.

2. Add the ingredients for your chosen parcel to the bowl and mix everything together, along with a pinch of salt and pepper.

3. Put a quarter of the ingredients into the middle of a 30cm square sheet of foil, then bring two opposite sides of foil together and seal down the middle. Fold the other two sides in to make a square or rectangular parcel, as flat as possible, but tightly closed at the edges. The parcel should be about the size of an A5 piece of paper. Repeat with the remaining 3 portions of ingredients.

❄ *Ice Kitchen Tip*
Any leftover onion or garlic can be thinly sliced or chopped and flash-frozen in a single layer on a covered tray, then put into a labelled resealable freezer bag, to be used in cooking straight from frozen.

FREEZE:
Place the parcels in the freezer until solid.

FREEZER TO TABLE:
Put the parcel into an oven preheated to 200°C/180°C fan/Gas Mark 6 for about 45 minutes until cooked through and piping hot.

Swift Salvation Sauces

Remember those flavoured sauce jars of Chicken Tonight ...?

Here is a MAHOOSIVE upgrade for you, although they are not just for chicken, mind you. Throw in veg, meatballs, pork strips, prawns, seafood, pasta, rice. Basically these are all sauces that can make meals out of random bits in your kitchen! Pure sauce(ry) ...

Tomato Sauce

SERVES 8 (4 FOR NOW AND 4 FOR LATER) • 5 MINUTES PREP • 25 MINUTES COOKING

This is my tomato sauce staple. I thicken it to spread on pizzas, use it as a base for pasta or for very simple tomato soup beginnings. Make it your own. If you have fussy eaters, bung a load of carrots, courgettes, spinach and peppers in there and blitz it together for a wonderful hidden vegetable sauce.

- 6 generous glugs of extra-virgin olive oil, plus a little extra
- 5 large garlic cloves, smashed
- 2 large bunches of basil, leaves picked and torn (reserve a few leaves to garnish)
- 1kg cherry tomatoes on the vine, or baby plum tomatoes

TRY ADDING:

— **Mediterranean vegetables (aubergine, courgette or spinach) – just simmer over a low heat until cooked through**

SWAP THE BASIL FOR:

— *1 tbsp ground cumin, 1 tbsp dried oregano and 2 tsp chilli powder for a Mexican base*
— *2 tbsp ras el hanout for a Moroccan base*
— *2 tbsp Cajun seasoning for a Creole base*

1. Heat the oil in a saucepan over a medium heat and add the garlic and basil, stirring continuously until the aromas fill the air, for a minute or so.

2. Add the tomatoes, lower the heat, cover and simmer for about 20 minutes, stirring often. Remove the lid and simmer for a few minutes more, to thicken. Finish with a little glug more of olive oil and season with salt and pepper to taste.

HOW TO USE

- Simply toss through just-cooked pasta and flurry over some grated Parmesan cheese.
- Add 500ml vegetable stock and blitz with a hand blender to make a lovely tomato soup that can easily become a base for further vegetable soups (add peppers and carrots and simmer until the vegetables are tender, then blitz again, season with salt and pepper to taste and serve).
- Add one of the spice mix suggestions to make a great flavoured base for world-inspired stews, casseroles, soups and sauces. Try adding sausages and beans to the ras el hanout Moroccan base, covering with a lid and simmering until the sausages are cooked through.
- Cook longer in step 2 to reduce and thicken to make a great pizza base sauce (see Freezer Pizza, page 68).

FREEZE:
Allow to cool completely, then pour into ice-cube trays, cover and put into the freezer; once frozen transfer to resealable freezer bags. Or portion up (I like preparing portions of two) and lay flat to freeze in labelled resealable freezer bags until solid.

FREEZER TO TABLE:
Put into a lidded saucepan with an extra splash of water, then place over a low heat until defrosted. Increase the heat and cook until piping hot through. Or defrost overnight in the fridge, before reheating on the hob.

Coconut Curry Sauce

SERVES 8 (4 FOR NOW AND 4 FOR LATER) • 15 MINUTES PREP • 25 MINUTES COOKING

We are a nation of curry lovers. This is quite possibly the simplest curry sauce for you to have at your fingertips. Keep it portioned out in the freezer, along with frozen strips of chicken, frozen fish, frozen prawns or sweet potato and veg, so you can avoid that last-minute takeaway and have something proudly homemade, with all the bang of your usual curry house but the ease of simply opening your freezer drawer.

2 large glugs of vegetable oil

2 onions, finely chopped

3 garlic cloves, finely chopped

3 heaped tbsp curry powder

3 tbsp garam masala

2 tbsp ground cumin

2 x 400g tins chopped tomatoes

2 x 400ml tins coconut milk

1 bird's-eye chilli, left whole, to serve

TRY ADDING:

— 2 tbsp garam masala for a richer flavour

— 1–2 tsp chilli powder for a kick

— whole bird's-eye chillies or dried chillies for a bigger kick

1. Heat the oil in a large saucepan over a medium heat, then add the onions, stirring regularly until softened and browned, about 10 minutes.

2. Add the garlic, curry powder, garam masala and ground cumin, stirring continuously until the aroma hits, for 20 seconds or so. Add the chopped tomatoes and the coconut milk, along with a pinch of salt and pepper. Increase the heat, bring to the boil, then simmer for a few minutes until thick and sauce-like.

HOW TO USE

This is a great base to make quick curries; just add a tin of drained chickpeas, a handful of spinach and frozen (or fresh) chicken strips, or frozen (or fresh) chunks of white fish or seafood (prawns work well!) or more vegetables (such as cauliflower florets, aubergine cubes and diced sweet potato). Increase the heat so it begins to boil, then immediately reduce to the lowest heat, cover and simmer until the veg and chicken are cooked through. Serve with cooked rice and flatbreads (see page 135).

 FREEZE:
Allow to cool completely, then pour into ice-cube trays, cover and put into the freezer; once frozen transfer to resealable freezer bags. Or portion up (I like preparing portions of two) and lay flat to freeze in labelled resealable freezer bags until solid.

FREEZER TO TABLE:
Put into a covered saucepan with an extra splash of water and place over a low heat until defrosted, then increase the heat and cook until piping hot through. Or defrost overnight in the fridge, before reheating on the hob.

Everything Sauce

SERVES 8 (4 FOR NOW AND 4 FOR LATER) • 10 MINUTES PREP • 20 MINUTES COOKING

Line up, line up ... Do you need an amazing everything sauce that can be a base for pies, soups, stews, casseroles? Go for this one. It can transform veg and meat and turn anything into a meal.

2 glugs of oil

3 onions, finely chopped

4 carrots, finely chopped

4 garlic cloves, finely chopped

2 tbsp finely chopped parsley leaves

2 heaped tbsp plain flour

2 vegetable stock cubes, crumbled

TRY ADDING:
— lardons or chopped bacon at step 1

1. Heat the oil in a large saucepan over a medium heat, add the onions and carrots and cook, stirring regularly until softened, about 10 minutes. Add the garlic and parsley, stirring continuously until the aroma hits, for 30 seconds or so.

2. Whisk in the flour and stock cubes, until the flour disappears, then gradually stir in about 500ml just-boiled water. Reduce the heat to low, cover and simmer, stirring often, until the carrots are soft, about 10–15 minutes. Season with salt and pepper to taste.

HOW TO USE

• To make a lovely base for soup, add 500ml–1 litre water then a couple of handfuls of veg (peas, potatoes and leeks work well), a couple of handfuls of chicken strips (frozen or fresh) and a splash of milk or cream. Bring to the boil, then reduce to a simmer and cook through. Season with salt and pepper to taste.

• For a gorgeously rich chicken casserole or base for a pastry-topped pot pie, add a splash of milk or cream, a couple of handfuls of veg (frozen peas, potatoes and leeks) and a couple of handfuls of chicken strips (frozen or fresh) and bring to the boil. Reduce to a simmer and cook until the chicken and veg are cooked and the liquid has reduced to make a rich sauce. Season to taste.

FREEZE:
Allow to cool completely, then pour into ice-cube trays, cover and freeze; once solid, transfer to resealable freezer bags. Or portion up (I like preparing portions of two) and lay flat to freeze in labelled resealable freezer bags.

FREEZER TO TABLE:
Put into a lidded saucepan with an extra splash of water, then place over a low heat until defrosted. Increase the heat and cook until piping hot through. Or defrost overnight in the fridge before reheating on the hob.

Ice Cube Sauces & Butters

Get your ice-cube trays out. I guarantee your future self will thank you for having a freezer stocked with cubes of different sauces, butters and dressings ready to go, to jazz up the simplest midweek meal from a basic bit of meat, fish, veg or salad, to a tongue-tantilising experience. Freeze them in ice-cube portions, then pop out (I reckon about 1–2 per person for sauces and 1 per person for butters) and store in labelled resealable freezer bags. Leave the cubes to defrost at room temperature whilst you get on with the other elements of your meal, then top with your choice of butter, or mix through the sauce or dressing.

Ice Cube Honey Mustard

SERVES 8 · 5–10 MINUTES PREP

Honey and mustard are undeniable partners; this dressing gives you that winning combination of sweet, sharp, sour and salt in an easy-to-use ice cube. And you thought that a midweek salad couldn't get any easier …

4 tbsp Dijon mustard

4 tbsp runny honey

4 garlic cloves, grated or crushed

4 tbsp olive oil

4 tbsp white wine vinegar

1. Mix together all the ingredients until well combined, either by whisking in a bowl or shaking together in a jar with a tight-fitting lid. Season with salt and pepper to taste.

HOW TO USE

• As a sauce for sausages and mash, or roast chicken.
• As a dressing for a simple salad of green leaves, walnuts, avocado and sugar snap peas.

Ice Cube Nuoc Cham

SERVES 8–12 · 5–10 MINUTES PREP

Quite possibly my fave of the ice cube sauces, this fiery Vietnamese dressing with its perfect elements of salt, sweet, sour and spice is liquid gold for tossing through a cold rice noodle salad with a little grilled chicken, shellfish and/or lots of raw crunchy veg. Pure summer day delight.

8 tbsp fish sauce

2 tsp dark brown sugar

4 garlic cloves, peeled

2–5 bird's-eye chillies (depending on how hot you like it!)

juice of 4 limes

1 stick of lemongrass, finely chopped

1. Pop all the ingredients into a food processor and blend until everything is finely chopped. Season to taste. Pop into ice-cube trays and freeze until solid. Pop out as required and thaw overnight in the fridge, or at room temperature.

HOW TO USE

• As a dipping sauce for spring rolls, or crispy fried seafood, like soft-shell crab or other fresh crab.
• As a dressing for a noodle salad.

Ice Cube Ginger Peanut

SERVES 8 • 5 MINUTES PREP

Transform your bog-standard stir-fry with the addition of this absolute beauty. I always prepare a batch chilli-free as it's a hit with kids and my eldest would happily bath open-mouthed in it, plus it's great for a quick throw-together meal in minutes. Let's not forget its 'dippability': such an impressive little number to whip out for dipping grilled meats and crunchy veg into.

4 tbsp peanut butter

2 thumb-sized piece of ginger

4 tbsp lime juice

4 tbsp brown sugar

2–4 bird's-eye chillies, (depending on how hot you like it)

4 tsp coriander leaves, finely chopped

2 garlic cloves

1. Pop all the ingredients into a food processor and blend until finely chopped. Season to taste. Pop into ice-cube trays and freeze until solid. Pop out as required and thaw overnight in the fridge, or at room temperature.

HOW TO USE

• As a dipping sauce for grilled chicken, pork or beef chunks on skewers, or strips.
• As a sauce for a stir-fry, adding vegetables and chicken, see Easiest Veg Stir-fry (page 93).

FREEZE:
Pour into ice-cube trays, cover and freeze until solid, then transfer to labelled resealable freezer bags.

FREEZER TO TABLE:
Remove from the freezer and defrost overnight in the fridge, or at room temperature to use immediately.

Pesto Mathematics

SERVES 8 • 10 MINUTES PREP

I have always loved a pesto. It really is a quick fix for so many things: pasta and gnocchi, yes, but also spooned over a hot baked potato, stirred through polenta, or mixed through grilled Mediterranean vegetables. I like to mess around with different combinations of leaf and nut, so this recipe is a handy one-stop shop for you to experiment with.

50g (2 small packets) leafy herbs, such as basil, coriander, parsley, rocket

2 garlic cloves, finely chopped

6 tbsp (about 60g) nuts, such as pine nuts, cashew nuts, walnuts or almonds

50g Parmesan cheese, grated

150g olive oil

4 tbsp lemon or lime juice

TRY ADDING:
— chopped sundried tomatoes
— chilli flakes (works beautifully with coriander)
— chopped black olives

SWAP FOR OR MIX THE LEAFY HERB WITH:
— *leafy carrot tops*
— *cooked broccoli florets*

COMBINATIONS TO TRY

basil + pine nut + lemon

coriander + cashew nut + lime

parsley + walnut + lemon

rocket + almond + lemon

1. Put the leaves, garlic, nuts and Parmesan into a food processor and pulse until combined but still a little chunky. Mix in the olive oil and citrus juice. Season with salt and pepper to taste.

HOW TO USE
- Slather over chicken breasts or white fish or salmon fillets. Place on a baking tray, cover with foil and bake in an oven preheated to 200°C/180°C fan/Gas Mark 6 for about 15 minutes until cooked through.
- Cut peppers, courgettes, aubergines, red onion and butternut squash into chunks. Tip onto a baking tray, stir through the pesto and a little salt and pepper and roast in an oven preheated to 200°C/180°C fan/Gas Mark 6 for about 30 minutes until golden and soft.
- Mix a few tablespoons of pesto through mashed potato or cooked polenta.
- Toss through hot pasta.

FREEZE:
Put into ice-cube trays, cover and freeze until solid, then transfer to labelled resealable freezer bags.

FREEZER TO TABLE:
Remove from the freezer and defrost overnight in the fridge, or at room temperature to use immediately.

Ice Cube Chimichurri

SERVES 8–12 • 15 MINUTES PREP

How often do you find yourself with a fridge full of limp-looking herbs and a lack of inspiration? There are so many things you can do with them – this South American-inspired recipe is a great way to turn them into a fantastic dressing to drizzle over barbecued or grilled meats – it works especially well with steak, chicken and fish – and over roasted vegetables, particularly sweet potatoes, or try it as a dressing over a tomato salad. See opposite for more information about freezing herbs, so you can always have at your fingertips a sprinkle of parsley, coriander or whichever herb takes your fancy!

2 small shallots, finely chopped

5 garlic cloves, finely chopped

4 small bunches (about 100g) of coriander leaves, finely chopped

4 small bunches (about 100g) of parsley leaves, finely chopped

1–4 small red chillies, deseeded and finely chopped

500ml extra-virgin olive oil

juice of 4 lemons

1. Whisk together all the ingredients until well combined and season with salt and pepper to taste.

 FREEZE:
Fill up your ice-cube trays, cover and freeze until solid, then transfer to a labelled resealable freezer bag and return to the freezer until needed.

 FREEZER TO TABLE:
Defrost in the fridge, or defrost at room temperature and use immediately.

Freezing Herbs

Freeze your leftover herbs by roughly chopping them and flash-freezing on a covered tray. Transfer to a labelled resealable freezer bag (use a different one for each herb). You can then add them straight to cooked dishes as they don't need to be defrosted first.

Don't forget that you can also freeze the stems of soft herbs like parsley and coriander; just finely chop or blitz them and make a paste with a little olive oil, then freeze them in ice-cube trays. These work wonderfully in soups and stews and reduce waste!

Frozen herbs work best in meals that need to be cooked, rather than as garnishes.

Freezing Citrus

Citrus fruits like lemons and limes can be frozen whole and defrosted under warm running water for a few seconds.

Although you can freeze slices or wedges of citrus fruit, they tend to dry out, so if I have an excess of lemons and limes I often freeze the juice and zest separately (especially when some recipes call for one or the other) in ice-cube trays before transferring to labelled resealable freezer bags once solid.

Zesting citrus fruits when frozen is slightly easier than when fresh.

Ice Cube Jerk Marinade

SERVES 8–12 · 10 MINUTES PREP

Rub over chicken, meats, fish and veg before grilling, frying or baking. Add a few teaspoons to a BBQ sauce, beans and stews for extra tropical oomph!

4 tsp allspice berries, toasted

½ cinnamon stick, broken into shards and toasted

1 tsp coriander seeds, toasted

2 tsp fresh thyme leaves

4 spring onions, roughly chopped

½–1 Scotch bonnet pepper, deseeded if you want less heat

3 garlic cloves

1 tsp grated nutmeg

3 tbsp demerara sugar

juice of 1 lime

½ tsp soy sauce

2 tsp oil

1. Put all the ingredients into a food processor and blitz until you have a smoothish paste. Season with salt and pepper to taste.

❄ *Ice Kitchen Tip*
Any leftover woody herbs, like thyme, can be frozen whole in resealable freezer bags to be used in cooking.

 FREEZE:
Pour into ice-cube trays, cover and freeze until solid, then transfer to labelled resealable freezer bags.

 FREEZER TO TABLE:
Remove from the freezer and defrost overnight in the fridge, or at room temperature to use immediately.

Buffalo Ice Cube Butter

SERVES 8–12 • 5 MINUTES PREP

Melt onto grilled or fried (decadent, I know!) chicken, try on Winger Winger Chicken Wings Dinner (see page 151) or serve with crudités and crumbled blue cheese.

250g unsalted butter, at room temperature

2 garlic cloves, crushed

2 tbsp white wine or cider vinegar

10 tbsp Frank's hot sauce (or other sour hot sauce)

large pinch of sea salt

large pinch of cracked black pepper

1. Beat the butter in a bowl with a wooden spoon until light and fluffy.

2. Add the remaining ingredients and mix together until well combined.

Tomato Basil Ice Cube Butter

SERVES 8–12 • 5 MINUTES PREP

Melt onto grilled meats, warm breads, use instead of oil or plain butter to pan-fry fish fillets, melt over cooked warm vegetables or try mixed into Loaded Potato Skins (see page 145).

250g unsalted butter, at room temperature

2 tbsp finely chopped sundried tomatoes

20 basil leaves, finely shredded

large pinch of sea salt

large pinch of cracked black pepper

1. Beat the butter in a bowl with a wooden spoon until light and fluffy.

2. Add the remaining ingredients and mix together until well combined.

 FREEZE:
Fill ice-cube trays with the butter, cover and freeze until solid. Once the cubes are frozen solid, pop them out and transfer to a labelled resealable freezer bag.

 FREEZER TO TABLE:
Pop out as required and defrost overnight in the fridge, or at room temperature to use immediately.

Blue Cheese Ice Cube Butter

SERVES 8–12 · 5 MINUTES PREP

Melt onto grilled meats, especially steak and chicken wings, or try mixed into Loaded Potato Skins (see page 145).

250g unsalted butter, at room temperature

100g crumbled blue cheese, e.g. Stilton

2 sprigs of thyme, leaves finely chopped

large pinch of sea salt

large pinch of cracked black pepper

1. Beat the butter in a bowl with a wooden spoon until light and fluffy.

2. Add the remaining ingredients and mix together until well combined.

Sriracha Lime Coriander Ice Cube Butter

SERVES 8–12 · 5 MINUTES PREP

Melt onto grilled or fried (decadent, I know!) meats, such as my Winger Winger Chicken Wings Dinner (see page 151), use instead of oil or plain butter to pan-fry fish fillets or try mixed into Loaded Potato Skins (see page 145).

250g unsalted butter, at room temperature

zest of 2 limes, plus a squeeze of the juice

2 tbsp sriracha (or 1 red chilli, deseeded and finely chopped)

2 tbsp finely chopped coriander leaves

large pinch of sea salt

large pinch of cracked black pepper

1. Beat the butter in a bowl with a wooden spoon until light and fluffy.

2. Add the remaining ingredients and mix together until well combined.

Cinna-berry Ice Cube Butter

SERVES 8–12 • 5 MINUTES PREP

Use on Cinna-berry Pancakes on page 26, or on hot toast, pancakes, French toast or desserts.

250g unsalted butter, at room temperature

2 tsp demerara sugar

2 tsp ground cinnamon

2 small handfuls of berries (fresh or defrosted from frozen), crushed

1 tsp vanilla extract

large pinch of sea salt

1. Beat the butter in a bowl with a wooden spoon until light and fluffy.

2. Add the remaining ingredients and mix together until well combined.

 FREEZE:
Fill ice-cube trays with the butter, cover and freeze until solid. Once the cubes are frozen solid, pop them out and transfer to a labelled resealable freezer bag.

 FREEZER TO TABLE:
Pop out as required and defrost overnight in the fridge, or at room temperature to use immediately.

Snacks & Sharers

The recipes in this chapter could be meals in their own right, but they have been so handy to crack out mid-afternoon or early evening, when guests turn up at the last minute for a nibble with a glass (or three) of wine; they are equally handy when my big boy gets home from nursery and is wanting something other than oaty bars. Have a whole drawer devoted to these – you can thank me later. As before, the chapter is divided into the time it takes to make the original recipe from first chop to table.

QUICK (30 MINUTES OR LESS)
Falafel

Spiced Flatbreads

Lamb, Cherry & Pine Nut Meatballs

Cookies & Cream Smoothie

MEDIUM (45 MINUTES OR LESS)
Jalapeño Corn Humitas

Polenta Chips

Cornbread

The Simplest Sausage Rolls

Bacon Cheese Straws

LONGER (45 MINUTES PLUS)
Thai Crab Cakes

Loaded Potato Skins

Korean Caulifower Poppers

Winger Winger Chicken Wings Dinner

Crispy Aubergine with Honey-Tamarind Drizzle

Falafel

MAKES 40 (20 FOR NOW AND 20 FOR LATER) • 15 MINUTES PREP • 10 MINUTES COOKING

Just as meatballs deserve a space in the freezer, falafel have earned their place in mine too. You can easily throw a meal together with a handful of these crowd-pleasers – they really need no further introduction.

4 x 400g tins chickpeas

1 large onion, finely chopped

5 garlic cloves, finely chopped

large bunch of parsley, leaves finely chopped

2½ tbsp ground cumin

2½ tbsp ground coriander

8 tbsp plain flour

vegetable oil, for frying

1. Drain the chickpeas, then pat dry with kitchen paper. Pulse them in a food processor until a coarse mixture is formed.

2. Add the remaining ingredients, except the vegetable oil, and add some salt and pepper. Pulse until the mixture is well combined. Use your hands to form the mixture into small patties about 1cm thick.

3. Heat a glug of oil in a large frying pan over a medium-low heat and fry the falafel for 2–3 minutes on each side until golden and cooked through. Drain briefly on a plate lined with kitchen paper and serve.

→ **Try with** flatbreads, hummus and crunchy veg, like cucumber, peppers and radishes.

FREEZE:
Cool completely, then place them on a tray, cover with foil and put them into the freezer to flash-freeze. As soon as they are frozen, place in a labelled resealable freezer bag.

FREEZER TO TABLE:
Transfer to a baking tray, cover with foil and bake in an oven preheated to 200°C/180°C fan/Gas Mark 6 for 20–30 minutes until piping hot through, removing the foil for the last 5 minutes of cooking.

Spiced Flatbreads

MAKES 8–10 · 15 MINUTES PREP · 10 MINUTES COOKING

Never buy supermarket flatbreads ever, ever again. You really won't want to after making this super-simple recipe and storing them ready to go in the freezer. Start with this version, then add different herbs and spices to tailor them to your dishes. I have them with EVERYTHING: soups, hummus, dips, curries ... I sometimes leave out the cumin and coriander leaves and eat them straight from the oven, glistening with Tomato Basil Ice Cube Butter (see page 127) for a Mediterranean feel.

400g self-raising flour, sifted, plus extra for dusting

400g yoghurt

1½ tsp baking powder

1 tsp ground cumin

1 tbsp chopped coriander leaves

butter, for brushing

SWAP THE CUMIN AND CORIANDER FOR:

— *pinch of chilli powder*

— *pinch of ground coriander*

— *pinch of Baharat seasoning*

— *pinch of Cajun seasoning*

— *any freshly chopped herbs*

1. Put all the ingredients, except the butter, in a bowl along with a little salt and pepper and use a spoon to mix together, then bring it all together with your hands.

2. Knead for a few minutes on a clean, flour-dusted surface then divide the dough into 8–10 balls and press into flatbreads about the thickness of a £2 coin.

3. Place a griddle pan or a dry frying pan over a high heat. Add a couple of flatbreads to the pan and cook for about 1 minute on each side, until puffed and golden, or charred by the ridges of the griddle pan. Repeat with the remaining flatbreads, cooking in batches that fit the pan. Brush half of the cooked flatbreads with a little butter, but leave the rest unbuttered, for freezing. Serve the buttered flatbreads.

 FREEZE:
Allow the unbuttered flatbreads to cool completely, then put them into a resealable freezer bag, separated by layers of baking parchment.

 **FREEZER TO TABLE:**
Brush each flatbread with a little butter (try one of the flavoured butters on pages 127–129), wrap in foil and put into an oven preheated to 200°C/180°C fan/Gas Mark 6 for about 10 minutes. Or defrost overnight in the fridge and halve the oven timings.

Lamb, Cherry & Pine Nut Meatballs

MAKES ABOUT 40 (JUST SMALLER THAN GOLF-BALL SIZE) • 15 MINUTES PREP • 10 MINUTES COOKING

Let's face it, as divine as meatballs are, making them during the week can be a bit of a faff. So commit yourself to making them in bulk at the weekend and then indulge in them whenever you fancy. By all means make and freeze meatballs using your favourite pork or beef recipe, but do give this fragrant spiced beauty, inspired by my friend and ex-neighbour Sabrina Ghayour, a go too. Perfect with harissa-streaked hummus, flatbreads and a tabbouleh salad. It's also fun with a tomato sauce jazzed up with a tablespoon of harissa. Think of this as a variation on your usual spaghetti and meatballs.

800g–1kg lamb mince

2 small onions, finely chopped

4 garlic cloves, finely chopped

8 heaped tbsp dried sour cherries (about 60g)

150g pine nuts, toasted and finely chopped

2 tsp ground cumin

1 tsp ground allspice

large bunch of parsley, leaves finely chopped

large bunch of mint, leaves finely chopped

4 eggs, beaten

zest of ½ lemon

vegetable oil, for frying

1. Mix together all the ingredients except the oil, in a large bowl with a pinch of salt and pepper, being careful not to overmix. Shape into about 40 balls.

2. Heat a large glug of oil in a large frying pan over a medium-low heat and fry the meatballs until golden brown on all sides, about 10–15 minutes. Transfer to a plate lined with kitchen paper to absorb any excess oil, then serve.

→ **Try with** hummus, flatbreads (see page 135) and tabbouleh.

❄ **Ice Kitchen Tip**
Any leftover lemon zest and juice can be frozen separately in ice-cube trays (covered), then transferred to labelled resealable freezer bags once frozen solid.

 FREEZE:
Cool completely, then place them on a tray, cover with foil and put them into the freezer to flash-freeze. As soon as they are solid, transfer to a labelled resealable freezer bag.

 FREEZER TO TABLE:
Put the frozen meatballs on a baking tray, cover with foil and bake in an oven preheated to 200°C/180°C fan/Gas Mark 6 for 20–30 minutes until piping hot through, removing the foil for the last 5 minutes of cooking. Or defrost overnight in the fridge and halve the oven timings.

Cookies & Cream Smoothie

SERVES 8 (4 FOR NOW AND 4 FOR LATER) • 5 MINUTES PREP

We all know that smoothies are a great way to boost your fruit and veg intake, as well as use up produce that is slightly past its best. Along with banana bread, this is how I like to use up blackened bananas, plus it tastes like milkshake. Sometimes if I have a little spinach getting a tad soggy I shove a small handful into this for added goodness (shh, don't tell Mr R.). You really won't be able to taste it!

8 small ripe bananas (the riper the better)

8 tbsp almond butter (or other nut butter)

8 heaped tbsp cacao nibs (or 6 tbsp cocoa powder)

2 tsp ground cinnamon

2 small handfuls of chopped dates

generous dash of vanilla extract (optional)

milk, to top up (try dairy, oat or any nut milk)

1. Put all the ingredients except the milk into a blender and blitz. Add just enough milk to get a smoothie consistency once blitzed again.

❊ *Ice Kitchen Tips*
- **Freeze your usual smoothie if you make too much of it, or blitz any fruit or milk that you can't use otherwise into a smoothie and freeze for another day. Great if you are about to go away on holiday and need to empty your fridge!**
- **Any leftover fruit (fresh or tinned) can be frozen in ready-portioned frozen fruit bags for smoothies, or flash-frozen on a covered tray and stored in labelled resealable freezer bags.**
- **If you have blackened bananas but can't get around to using them, peel, slice (or mash) and freeze to make Brown Sugar Banana Bread (see page 35) or add to ready-portioned bags of frozen fruit for smoothies.**

 FREEZE:
Portion up and freeze flat in labelled resealable bags.

 FREEZER TO TABLE:
Defrost the smoothie in the fridge.

Jalapeño Corn Humitas

SERVES 8 (4 FOR NOW AND 4 FOR LATER) • 15 MINUTES PREP • 25 MINUTES COOKING

Although I love a traditional humita (my mouth literally waters as I unwrap those husks), I really don't mind this lazy version: it tastes just as good and is so full of heady spiced flavour. Think of it as the love child of creamed corn and a spiced corn salsa.

6 tbsp butter

large bunch of spring onions, finely chopped

2 green peppers, deseeded and finely chopped

5 garlic cloves, finely chopped

8 tsp paprika

½ tsp cayenne pepper

1 tsp dried oregano

4 tomatoes, innards scooped out and discarded, diced

4 tbsp chopped coriander leaves

juice of 1 lime

2-4 tbsp jalapeño peppers, finely chopped

4 x 285g tins sweetcorn, drained

3 eggs

6 tbsp double cream

8 tbsp grated Parmesan cheese

1. Preheat the oven to 200°C/180°C fan/Gas Mark 6.

2. Melt the butter in a large frying pan over a medium heat, then add the spring onions and peppers, stirring regularly until softened, about 5-10 minutes. Add the garlic, paprika, cayenne pepper and dried oregano, stirring continuously, until the aromas hit you, for 20 seconds or so. Add the diced tomato, coriander, lime juice and jalapeno peppers and cook for another 5 minutes, stirring regularly.

3. In a food processor, blitz the sweetcorn with the eggs and cream, then pour this into the pan ingredients. Mix well and season with salt and pepper to taste.

4. Pour half the humita mixture into a shallow baking dish, and divide the rest into 4 individual foil packets For Later, and sprinkle over the Parmesan. Cover the baking dish with foil or fold the foil packets shut. Bake in the oven for 15 minutes, then serve.

→ **Try with** grilled meats, especially chicken and steak, or dunk in tortilla chips as a snack.

 FREEZE:
This is best frozen in individual foil packets, so allow to cool completely, then label and put into the freezer.

 FREEZER TO TABLE:
Put the foil packets on to a baking tray and bake in an oven preheated to 200°C/180°C fan/Gas Mark 6 for 30-45 minutes until piping hot through. Or defrost overnight in the fridge and halve the oven timings.

Polenta Chips

SERVES 8 (4 FOR NOW AND 4 FOR LATER) • 5 MINUTES PREP • 40 MINUTES COOKING

Although this is a clever way to use up leftover polenta (which I always seem to make too much of), polenta chips also deserve their own limelight. A different freezer chip worth having around – they make a pleasant change for anyone who loves the usual type. Serve with everything.

1 litre vegetable stock

300g quick-cook polenta, plus extra for dusting

4 tsp smoked paprika

4 tsp dried oregano

4 handfuls of grated Parmesan cheese

vegetable oil, for brushing

SWAP THE OREGANO AND PAPRIKA FOR:
— *generous pinch of chilli powder*
— *2 tsp ground cumin and 2 tsp ground coriander*
— *4 tsp Cajun seasoning*
— *2 heaped tsp harissa paste*
— *2 heaped tsp chipotle paste*
— *2 heaped tsp Jerk Marinade (shop-bought or see page 126)*

1. Pour the stock into a saucepan and place over a high heat. When it begins to boil, reduce the heat to low, then whisk in the polenta, whisking constantly. Add the paprika, oregano, Parmesan and a pinch of salt and pepper and continue whisking until thickened, about 10–15 minutes.

2. Grease and line a small baking dish with baking parchment. Pour the polenta into the lined dish and spread out so that it is about 1cm thick. Allow to cool completely, then chill in the fridge until solid. Meanwhile, preheat the oven to 220°C/200°C fan/Gas Mark 7.

3. When the polenta is firm, remove it from the dish and cut into chips (or any other shape you fancy). Sprinkle over the extra polenta, to dust the chips.

4. Put half the polenta chips on to a baking tray, brush with oil and bake in the oven for 30 minutes until crisp and golden, turning halfway through cooking, then serve.

 FREEZE:
Follow the recipe up to the end of step 3, then place the polenta chips in a single layer on a tray lined with baking parchment, cover with foil and put into the freezer to flash-freeze. When frozen, transfer to a labelled resealable freezer bag.

FREEZER TO TABLE:
Place the polenta chips in a single layer on a baking tray lined with baking parchment, cover with foil and bake in an oven preheated to 200°C/180°C fan/Gas Mark 6 for 40–50 minutes until cooked through, turning halfway through and uncovering for the last 5 minutes.

Cornbread

MAKES 12 (6 FOR NOW AND 6 FOR LATER) • 10 MINUTES PREP • 30 MINUTES COOKING

The colour, flavour and texture of this cornbread is pure sunshine, especially slathered with butter and honey. These ready-to-go versions are divine for breakfast with bacon and eggs, or try it with the delicious Creole Gumbo (see page 40) – a heaven-made match.

10 tbsp butter (about 150g), melted, plus extra for greasing and frying

4 spring onions, finely chopped

2 x 198g tins sweetcorn, drained (or use 400g frozen sweetcorn, defrosted)

1 red chilli, deseeded and finely chopped

300g quick-cook polenta

300g plain flour, sifted

4 tsp baking powder

large pinch of salt

300ml pot soured cream

4 eggs

200g milk

1. Preheat the oven to 200°C/180°C fan/Gas Mark 6 and grease two 6-hole muffin tins with a little melted butter.

2. Put about a tablespoon of the butter into a small frying pan over a medium heat; when it starts to foam add the spring onions, sweetcorn and chilli and fry, stirring often, until the sweetcorn is golden, about 5 minutes.

3. In a small bowl, mix together the polenta, flour, baking powder and salt.

4. In a large bowl, whisk the soured cream with the eggs, milk and remaining melted butter until smooth. Fold in the dry polenta mixture until you have a smooth batter, then divide between the holes in the muffin tins and bake in the oven for 25–30 minutes until golden and cooked through, then serve.

→ **Try with** salted butter and runny honey.

❄ *Ice Kitchen Tip*
Any leftover spring onions can be frozen whole or chopped and frozen in portions in ice-cube trays (covered), then popped out into a labelled resealable freezer bag.

FREEZER TO TABLE:
Put the foil-wrapped cornbread on a baking tray and bake in an oven preheated to 200°C/180°C fan/Gas Mark 6 for 20–30 minutes until piping hot through. Or defrost overnight in the fridge and halve the oven timings.

FREEZE:
Cool the cornbread muffins completely, double wrap in foil and place in a resealable freezer bag.

The Simplest Sausage Rolls

MAKES 20 (SMALL) (10 FOR NOW AND 10 FOR LATER) • 15 MINUTES PREP • 25 MINUTES COOKING

Proper sausage rolls with English mustard are the perfect little snack. As they are so easy to make (and the reason why I always keep pastry in the freezer!), I split the sausage meat and add a different flavouring to each bowl. Just remember to label each freezer bag so you don't end up playing sausage roll-ette ... unless that's your thing?

6 sausages (about 400g), meat squeezed from the casings (or use veggie sausages)

1 tbsp dried thyme

6 tbsp (about 50g) breadcrumbs

1 x 320g sheet of ready-rolled puff pastry (previously unfrozen if you are planning to freeze the unbaked sausage rolls)

1 egg, beaten

SWAP THE THYME FOR:
— *1 tbsp finely chopped sage leaves*
— *1 tbsp toasted cumin seeds*
— *1 tbsp toasted fennel seeds*
— *1 tbsp onion chutney*
— *1 tbsp Jerk Marinade (shop-bought or see page 126)*
— *1 tbsp hot English mustard*
— *1 tbsp hot chilli sauce*

1. Preheat the oven to 200°C/180°C fan/Gas Mark 6.

2. Mix the sausage meat with the thyme, breadcrumbs and a little salt and pepper. Divide the mixture into two balls.

3. Unroll the pastry sheet and slice it in half down its length to make 2 long strips.

4. Take one of the balls of sausage meat and roll it into a long cylinder to run the length of the pastry strip and position it slightly off-centre on one of the pastry strips. Brush the edges of the pastry with the beaten egg, fold over and seal, pressing down the edges with the fork. Brush the top of the roll with more beaten egg, then cut into about 10 rolls, or less if you prefer larger rolls. Repeat with the remaining sausage meat and pastry strip, but don't egg-wash them.

5. Transfer the egg-washed half to a baking tray lined with baking parchment and bake in the oven for about 25 minutes until golden, puffed up and cooked through. Serve with mustard and ketchup at the ready.

FREEZE:
Follow the recipe up to the end of step 4, but don't brush the top of the roll with beaten egg. Put the uncooked sausage rolls on to a baking tray lined with baking parchment. Once frozen, place the sausage rolls in a labelled resealable freezer bag.

FREEZER TO TABLE:
Place the sausage rolls on to a baking tray lined with baking parchment, brush with beaten egg and bake in an oven preheated to 200°C/180°C fan/Gas Mark 6 for 35–45 minutes.

Bacon Cheese Straws

MAKES 24 (12 FOR NOW AND 12 FOR LATER) • 15 MINUTES PREP • 15 MINUTES WAITING • 20 MINUTES COOKING

A step up from your regular version, the bacon adds, well, bacon-y perfection. You cannot go wrong with serving these as a pre-dinner snack with a glass of bubbles, or freezing ahead of a kid's birthday party. Yes, they are slightly retro, but it makes total sense. You can also always leave out the bacon for a classic straw.

2 x 320g sheets of previously unfrozen ready-rolled all-butter puff pastry (or use a block of pastry and roll into a 30cm square, about 5mm thick)

8 egg yolks, beaten

300g Cheddar cheese, grated

generous pinch of cayenne (or paprika, for a less spicy version)

24 rashers of streaky bacon

1. Lay out the pastry and brush all over with the egg yolk mixture. Sprinkle over the Cheddar and press lightly into the pastry, then sprinkle over the cayenne pepper.

2. Use the back of a knife to stretch the rashers of bacon slightly, so they are the same length as the pastry. Lay the rashers of bacon vertically down the pastry so you end up with bacon stripes. Use a sharp knife to slice the pastry into long strips so you end up with 12 untwisted straws with bacon running down their centres and a little pastry on each side of the bacon. Repeat with the second sheet of pastry.

3. Twist each strip a few times to make a curly straw. Put on a baking tray lined with baking parchment, cover and chill in the fridge for about 15 minutes.

4. Meanwhile, preheat the oven to 220°C/200°C fan/ Gas Mark 7.

5. Bake the uncovered tray of straws in the oven for 20–25 minutes until risen and golden brown.

FREEZE:
Follow the recipe up to step 3. Lay the twisted straws on a baking tray lined with baking parchment and cover, then put into the freezer until frozen solid. Transfer to a resealable freezer bag.

FREEZER TO TABLE:
Put the cheese straws on a baking tray lined with parchment and bake in an oven preheated to 190°C/170°C fan/Gas Mark 5 for 20–25 minutes until golden brown and risen.

Thai Crab Cakes

MAKES ABOUT 16 (8 FOR NOW AND 8 FOR LATER) • 15 MINUTES PREP • 30 MINUTES WAITING
5 MINUTES COOKING

Crab or fish cakes are a must-have in any well-stocked freezer. To know that when you get home after a tiring day you can pop a few into the oven and sit back and wait until you are transported to some salty ocean location with each bite, is nothing short of bliss. These are also one of my son's favourite post-nursery snacks (beats a rice cake I guess!).

500g cooked white crab meat

2 tbsp chopped coriander leaves

juice of 1 lime

zest of 2 limes

2 red chillies, finely chopped (remove the seeds if you want milder heat)

2.5cm piece of fresh ginger, peeled and grated

4 tsp sweet chilli sauce

4 medium potatoes, peeled, boiled and mashed

4 spring onions, finely chopped

2 eggs, beaten

5 tbsp plain flour, plus extra for coating

vegetable oil, for frying

SWAP THE CRAB, CORIANDER, LIME, CHILLI, GINGER AND SWEET CHILLI SAUCE FOR:

— cooked flaked salmon, peas, parsley and lemon

— flaked smoked mackerel, horseradish, dill and lemon

— cooked flaked cod, sweet potato, cayenne pepper, paprika, and lime

1. Preheat the oven to 200°C/180°C fan/Gas Mark 6.

2. Mix together all the ingredients, except the vegetable oil. Season with salt and pepper to taste and put into the fridge to firm up for about 30 minutes.

3. Form the mixture into 16 cakes, then dredge each one in flour and set aside.

4. Heat a generous glug of vegetable oil in a large frying pan over a medium heat and fry the crab cakes for 3–5 minutes, turning halfway through, so both sides are golden brown. Drain briefly on kitchen paper and serve.

➜ **Try with** a crunchy, zesty salad (think carrots, cucumber, lettuce, cabbage and lime) and more sweet chilli sauce for dipping.

 FREEZE:
Cool completely, then place the crab cakes on a tray, cover with foil and put them into the freezer to flash-freeze. Once frozen place in a labelled resealable freezer bag.

FREEZER TO TABLE:
Transfer the crab cakes to a baking tray, cover with foil and bake in an oven preheated to 200°C/180°C fan/Gas Mark 6 for 30–45 minutes until piping hot through, removing the foil for the last 5 minutes. Or defrost overnight in the fridge and halve the oven timings.

Loaded Potato Skins

MAKES 16 (8 FOR NOW AND 8 FOR LATER) • 10 MINUTES PREP • 1¼ HOURS COOKING

A great sharing food for sofa Sundays (and movie nights, generally) but equally good with ribs, barbecues and summer get-togethers. Make a platter of these skins and lay out a variety of different toppings (think chillies, kimchi, shredded chicken, pulled pork (see page 78) so your diners can pile on their own flavour combinations. You could even do this with sweet potatoes, and fill the skins with Lentil Chilli Non-Carne (see page 44).

8 large baking potatoes

oil, for rubbing

200g grated Cheddar cheese

150g pot soured cream

4 spring onions, finely chopped

8 rashers of streaky bacon, fried until crisp and then crumbled

4 tsp American mustard

ADD:

— Jerk Marinade (see page 126)

— Buffalo Ice Cube Butter (see page 127)

— cooked and shredded chicken

SWAP THE CHEDDAR AND BACON FOR:

— *blue cheese and bacon*

— *tuna and sweetcorn*

1. Preheat the oven to 200°C/180°C fan/Gas Mark 6.

2. Rub the potatoes in oil, place on a baking tray and bake for about 50 minutes–1 hour until crisp-skinned but fluffy on the inside.

3. Allow the potatoes to cool, then slice in half lengthways and carefully scoop out the innards, popping them into a bowl, leaving a 1cm layer of potato in the skins.

4. Add the Cheddar to the bowl of potato (reserving a good handful for topping), the soured cream, spring onions, bacon (reserving a little for topping) and the mustard. Mix together and season with salt and pepper to taste. Spoon the mixture back into the skins, then sprinkle over the reserved Cheddar and bacon.

5. Return the skins to the baking tray and bake in the oven for another 15–20 minutes until golden and bubbling on top, then serve.

FREEZE:
Cool completely, then place them on a tray, cover and put into the freezer to flash-freeze. As soon as they are frozen solid, place in a resealable freezer bag.

FREEZER TO TABLE:
Empty into a lidded saucepan, on a low to medium heat, breaking up as it defrosts. When fully defrosted, add a splash of water, increase the heat and cook, stirring often, until piping hot through. Or defrost overnight in the fridge, before reheating on the hob as set out.

Korean Cauliflower Poppers

MAKES 40 (20 FOR NOW AND 20 FOR LATER) • 20 MINUTES PREP • 30 MINUTES WAITING
30 MINUTES COOKING

Poppers make such great party bites, especially flavour-bombs like these ones. The gochujang works so unbelievably well with the cauliflower base. But don't wait for a party to serve these, try it with a crunchy side salad and some simple grilled chicken.

2 cauliflowers, chopped into 1cm chunks (don't worry if a lot of it crumbles)

vegetable oil, for drizzling

3 generous knobs of butter

4 spring onions, finely chopped

6 heaped tbsp plain flour, plus extra for coating

1 litre milk

200g grated Cheddar cheese

2 tbsp gochujang paste

4 eggs, beaten

panko breadcrumbs, for crumbing

1. Preheat the oven to 200°C/180°C fan/Gas Mark 6 and line a baking tray with baking parchment.

2. Place the cauliflower florets on another baking tray, drizzle with oil, toss to coat all the pieces, season with salt and pepper and bake for 15 minutes. Once cooled, blitz half of the cauliflower in a food processor and set the remaining florets aside.

3. Melt the butter in a large saucepan over a medium heat and fry the spring onions, stirring regularly until softened, about a couple of minutes. Whisk in the flour, then gradually whisk in the milk until thick, about 15 minutes. Stir in the Cheddar; the mixture should now be like a thick béchamel sauce.

4. Add the gochujang paste, along with the puréed cauliflower and the remaining florets. Mix well and season with salt and pepper to taste (the mixture should be really thick now). Allow to cool then empty the mixture into a dish, cover with foil, ensuring it touches the surface. Place the dish into the freezer for about 30 minutes until the mixture is cold and firm.

SWAP THE GOCHUJANG
PASTE FOR:
— *2 cubes Jerk Marinade
(see page 126)*
— *2 tbsp harissa paste*
— *2 tbsp chipotle paste*
— *4 tbsp Cajun seasoning*

5. In the meantime create a 'crumbing station' by putting the remaining flour, eggs and breadcrumbs into separate shallow bowls.

6. Form the cauliflower mixture into 40 balls. Dip each in the flour, then the egg and finally the breadcrumbs and set aside on a baking tray. (It will be messy but to avoid carnage use one hand for the flour and breadcrumbs and the other for the egg.)

7. Shallow-fry the poppers in vegetable oil in a large frying pan, turning regularly until golden brown, or use a deep-fryer, or heat the oil in a large saucepan to 180°C (or until a breadcrumb sizzles and turns golden immediately) and fry for a couple minutes. Pop fried poppers onto a plate lined with kitchen roll, then serve immediately.

FREEZE:
You can freeze the poppers before or after baking; simply place on a tray, cover with foil and put them into the freezer to flash-freeze. As soon as they are frozen, place in a labelled resealable freezer bag.

FREEZER TO TABLE:
Put in the fridge overnight; once defrosted, shallow-fry the poppers in vegetable oil in a large frying pan, turning regularly until golden brown, or use a deep-fryer, or heat the oil in a large saucepan to 180°C (or until a breadcrumb sizzles and turns golden immediately) and fry for a couple minutes. Pop fried poppers onto a plate lined with kitchen paper, then serve immediately.

Winger Winger Chicken Wings Dinner

SERVES 4–6 • 2 MINUTES PREP • 45 MINUTES COOKING

I am total sucker for a chicken wing, a dippy sauce and sticky fingers. I make sure that I always have chicken wings in my freezer drawer as well as a stock of frozen butters so I can scratch the itch whenever it appears – scratching, as you will see, couldn't be any simpler. The baking powder trick is a goody for crispy chicken.

1 tbsp baking powder

1kg frozen chicken wings

FLAVOUR IDEAS

— 2–4 tbsp (or a thick 5cm slice) of your choice of ice cube butter (see pages 121–129)

— 2–4 tbsp gochujang paste

— 2–4 tbsp chipotle paste mixed with 1 tbsp honey

— 2–4 tbsp BBQ sauce

— 2 tbsp butter mixed with 1 heaped tbsp Cajun seasoning

1. Preheat the oven to 200°C/180°C fan/Gas Mark 6.

2. Put the baking powder into a large freezer bag, add the wings and give them a good shake to ensure the wings are coated (you may need to do this in batches). Dust off any excess powder then place the coated wings on a baking sheet, in a single layer. Sprinkle over a little salt and pepper and bake for about 45–55 minutes, turning halfway, until cooked through.

3. Place under a hot grill for a few minutes so that the skin crisps up and becomes golden.

4. Before serving, toss the hot wings in a bowl with your chosen addition.

→ *Try with* salads and crudités.

Crispy Aubergine with Honey–Tamarind Drizzle

SERVES 8 (4 FOR NOW AND 4 FOR LATER) • 5 MINUTES PREP • 1 HOUR WAITING • 10 MINUTES COOKING

Is your mouth watering yet? Stock your freezer with crunchy aubs, people ... Amazing for dipping in a gazillion different kinds of sauces, like tzatziki or an aioli laced with chipotle paste. Before you go rogue, do at least try out this recipe once – the combination of honey and tamarind is perfection. I promise you will be back for more.

4 aubergines, cut into 5mm slices

2 litres milk, for soaking

4 large handfuls of polenta flour, for coating

½ tsp sea salt flakes

4 eggs, beaten

vegetable oil, for drizzling

FOR THE DRESSING

8 tbsp honey

4 tbsp tamarind paste

1 tsp Aleppo pepper flakes or chilli flakes

zest of 1 lime

TO SERVE (PER SERVING OF 4)

1 block of feta

1 tbsp chopped coriander leaves

1. Preheat the oven to 220°C/200°C fan/Gas Mark 7 and line a baking tray with baking parchment. Put the aubergine slices into a bowl and cover completely with the milk. Leave for about 1 hour to draw out any bitterness.

2. For the dressing, whisk together the honey and tamarind, add the Aleppo pepper and half the lime zest. Season with salt and pepper to taste and set aside.

3. Mix the polenta with a generous teaspoon of salt flakes. Set up a crumbing station, with the bowls of flour (add a generous pinch of salt and pepper), beaten egg and polenta. Dunk the aubergine into the flour, then the egg and finally the polenta and arrange on the lined baking sheet. It will be messy but to avoid carnage use one hand for the flour and polenta and the other for the egg. Lightly drizzle over a little oil and bake in the oven for 10–15 minutes until light golden, crispy and cooked through.

4. To serve, crumble over the feta, drizzle over the honey-tamarind dressing and scatter the coriander and remaining lime zest over the half For Now.

 FREEZE:
Follow the recipe up to the end of step 3 (leave making the dressing until the day you plan to serve the aubergine) and allow to cool completely. Arrange in a single layer on a tray, cover with foil and place in the freezer to flash-freeze. Once frozen, place the aubergine in a labelled resealable freezer bag.

FREEZER TO TABLE:
Place the aubergine on a lined baking sheet, cover with foil and bake in an oven preheated to 200°C/180°C fan/Gas Mark 6 for 20–25 minutes, removing the foil for the last 5 minutes, until crisp and piping hot throughout. Serve as detailed in step 4.

Puds & Cool Treats

This really needs no further introduction. A decadent selection of puds for when you want something warm out of the oven (just head to your freezer first) and nice icy treats that are so chilled (and meant to be!), to keep yourselves well stocked for all-year-round 'dessertion'. As with previous chapters, I've divided the Puds section into the time it takes to make the original recipe from first chop to table, for ease of reference.

PUDS

Quick (30 Minutes or Less)

Salted Caramel Ripple Cookie Dough

The Simplest Cookie

Berry Compote

Peach Puff Tart

Blueberry Turnovers

Longer (45 Minutes Plus)

Vanilla Cardamom Rice Pudding

Baked Berry Slump

COOL TREATS

Proper Ice Cream Sandwiches

No Churn Ice Cream

Oreo Peanut Butter Ice Cake

Frozen Yoghurt Bark

Watermelon Sherbet

Mango Mojito Granita

Fudgesicles

Popsicles

Instant Berry Fro-yo

Iced Berries & White Chocolate Sauce

Salted Caramel Ripple Cookie Dough

SERVES 8 (4 FOR NOW AND 4 FOR LATER) • 5 MINUTES PREP • 15 MINUTES COOKING

This cookie dough recipe is *purely* for cookie dough's sake – don't even think about baking this. It is totally safe to eat in its 'raw' state, and my word, will you want to! In fact, I've never managed to hold off eating it in its pure state to find out what it's like in ice cream, but I'm guessing pretty amazing.

400g plain flour

300g butter, at room temperature

240g soft light brown sugar

4 tsp vanilla extract

a generous pinch of salt

6 tbsp milk

a couple of handfuls of chocolate chips

6 tbsp salted caramel

SWAP THE CHOCOLATE CHIPS FOR:

— *hundreds and thousands*

— *chopped chocolate bars, Smarties or other sweets (like Rolos or Maltesers)*

1. Preheat the oven to 200°C/180°C fan/Gas Mark 6.

2. Spread the flour out on a large baking tray and bake in the oven for 15 minutes until toasted.

3. In a large bowl, beat together the butter and the sugar until light and fluffy. Add the vanilla extract, salt and the toasted flour. Keep beating while you gradually add the milk until you get a cookie dough texture.

4. Mix in the chocolate chips (or other treats), then swirl through the salted caramel. Enjoy mixed into ice creams, or straight from the bowl.

FREEZE:
Halve the cookie dough, then shape and roll each half into a compact cylinder, with a diameter of about 4-5cm. Wrap well in foil and put into the freezer. You can also roll into mini balls, flash-freeze on a covered baking sheet and then put into a labelled resealable freezer bag.

FREEZER TO TABLE:
Unwrap the frozen dough and use a knife to slice off what you require, or if freezing as cookie dough balls, simply take what you want from the freezer bag. Leave out at room temperature for about 5-10 minutes if you prefer a softer cookie dough, but you can also nibble and use from frozen!

The Simplest Cookie

MAKES ABOUT 20 COOKIES (10 FOR NOW AND 10 FOR LATER) • 5 MINUTES PREP • 10 MINUTES COOKING

A cookie is always a good idea, but a cookie fresh out of the oven is the best idea. So try it my way: make the dough, bake a few cookies but freeze the rest of the dough in an easy-to-slice cylinder so you can slice, bake and be eating freshly made cookies in a jiff, without the creaming and beating faff. Lazy deliciousness.

100g unsalted butter, at room temperature

150g soft light brown sugar

1 egg

dash of vanilla extract

200g self-raising flour, sifted with a large pinch of salt

TRY ADDING:

— handful of chocolate chips
— handful of colourful sprinkles or hundreds and thousands
— handful of fudge chunks
— handful of Smarties

1. Preheat the oven to 200°C/180°C fan/Gas Mark 6 and line a couple of large baking trays with baking parchment.

2. Cream the butter and sugar together, using a wooden spoon or electric mixer, until light and fluffy. Slowly beat in the egg, then the vanilla extract.

3. Fold the flour into the creamed butter and sugar, followed by any additions. Bring the dough into two balls.

4. Divide one dough ball into 10 small (or 5 large) balls. Flatten them slightly and then arrange on the lined baking trays, leaving plenty of space for them to spread out into cookies. Bake in the oven for about 10 minutes until golden and cooked through. Cool on a wire rack.

FREEZE:
Follow the recipe up to the end of step 3. Shape and roll the second half of the cookie dough into a compact cylinder, with a diameter of about 4–5cm. Wrap well in foil and place into the freezer.

FREEZER TO TABLE:
Unwrap the dough cylinder and use a knife to slice 5mm-thick slices of cookie dough (as many as you need!). Put on to a baking sheet and bake in an oven preheated to 200°C/180°C fan/Gas Mark 6 for about 15 minutes, or until golden and cooked through.

Berry Compote

SERVES 8 (4 FOR NOW AND 4 FOR LATER) • 5 MINUTES PREP • 10 MINUTES COOKING

Compotes are a great back-up to have in the kitchen to transform a host of breakfasts and desserts into something a little extra special. Try spooning over your porridge, Ice Kitchen Oats (see page 28), Cinna-berry Pancakes (see page 26) and waffles at breakfast time, or swirl it into your No Churn Ice Cream (see page 168). Eat with crumbled meringue and whipped cream for a quick Eton Mess, or swap the filling in your Blueberry Turnovers (see page 162). You can experiment with different spicing, but I always find myself coming back to warming cinnamon.

1kg frozen mixed berries

100–200g caster sugar (depending on how sweet you like it)

2 cinnamon sticks, broken in half

zest of 2 limes

SWAP THE CINNAMON FOR:

– *2 tsp vanilla extract*

– *1 tbsp finely chopped mint*

1. Put the berries, sugar, cinnamon sticks and lime zest into a saucepan, along with 3–4 tablespoons water. Bring to the boil, then reduce the heat and simmer for 5–10 minutes until thickened. Allow to cool before serving.

❄ *Ice Kitchen Tip*
   Any leftover citrus juice can be frozen in portions in ice-cube trays (covered), then popped out and stored in a labelled resealable freezer bag.

 **FREEZER TO TABLE:**
To defrost in the microwave, empty into a heatproof bowl, add a splash of water and cover with a lid. Defrost in short bursts on the defrost setting, stirring often to break it up. Or transfer to a small lidded saucepan, add a splash of water and defrost over a low heat, stirring often to break it up until fully defrosted. You can enjoy it cold, or increase the heat to warm it through, stirring often, if you fancy it that way. Or defrost overnight in the fridge, before reheating on the hob.

 FREEZE:
Allow to cool completely, then put into ice-cube trays, cover and freeze. Once frozen solid, pop out into a labelled resealable freezer bag.

Peach Puff Tart

SERVES 8 (4 FOR NOW AND 4 FOR LATER) • 10 MINUTES PREP • 20 MINUTES COOKING

Puff pastry deserves the highest praise for being able to give us the most glorious desserts with the most minimal effort. Amaretto and peach work so wonderfully together, especially with a dollop of mascarpone to serve. It is quite perfect for dinner parties.

6 large ripe peaches, thinly sliced

6 tbsp honey

generous dash of Amaretto, plus extra to serve

large pinch of ground cinnamon

2 ready-rolled (previously unfrozen) sheets of puff pastry, or 2 blocks of (previously unfrozen) puff pastry, rolled out to a thickness of 5mm

1 egg, beaten

SWAP THE PEACHES AND CINNAMON FOR:

— *peaches and lavender sprigs*

— *strawberries with a drizzle of balsamic glaze*

— *berries with star anise*

1. Preheat the oven to 220°C/200°C fan/Gas Mark 7 and put a baking tray in to heat up.

2. Mix the peach slices with the honey, Amaretto and cinnamon.

3. Lay the pastry sheets out on a sheet of baking parchment, pierce all over with a fork and lightly score a 1cm border. Brush the border of one sheet with the beaten egg.

4. Arrange the fruit in the middle of the pastry.

5. Slide the tart, on its baking parchment, on to the heated tray. Bake for 15–20 minutes until the pastry is puffed up and golden.

➜ **Try with** mascarpone and fresh mint leaves.

 FREEZE:
Follow the recipe up to the end of step 4, but don't brush the border with beaten egg. Flash-freeze on the lined baking tray; once frozen solid, wrap in foil, then label up and pop into your freezer file.

FREEZER TO TABLE:
Preheat the oven to 220°C/200°C fan/Gas Mark 7 and put a baking tray inside to heat up. Unwrap the tart, brush the border with beaten egg and transfer to the hot baking tray. Bake for about 20 minutes, or until the pastry is puffed up and golden.

Blueberry Turnovers

MAKES 12 (4 FOR NOW AND 8 FOR LATER) • 10 MINUTES PREP • 20 MINUTES COOKING

I'm not quite sure why you don't see turnovers around as much these days, but pass me a cold one filled with this moreish blueberry filling (thank goodness for frozen blueberries) and a cup of tea any day and I'm a happy gal. Also, they taste pretty wonderful hot and fresh out of the oven with a dollop of ice cream.

2 tbsp butter

800g bag frozen blueberries (or use fresh)

100g caster sugar

2 tbsp cornflour mixed with 2 tbsp water

2 tsp vanilla extract

zest of 2 lemons

flour, for dusting

2 x 375g packs of previously unfrozen puff pastry (or use ready-rolled sheets)

2 egg yolks

2 tbsp milk

demerara sugar, for sprinkling

SWAP THE BLUEBERRIES FOR:
— *any other frozen fruit filling, cherry is delicious!*

1. Preheat the oven to 200°C/180°C fan/Gas Mark 6 and line a baking sheet with baking parchment.

2. Melt the butter in a saucepan over a medium heat, then add the blueberries, sugar, cornflour mixture, vanilla and lemon zest. Increase the heat and cook until the blueberries have defrosted and the mixture becomes thick and compote-like, about 10 minutes, stirring now and again, then allow to cool.

3. Lightly dust a work surface with flour. Roll out the pastry into a rectangle about 5mm thick (or if using ready rolled, use as is) and use a sharp knife to cut into 12 squares.

4. Place 1 tablespoon of blueberry compote in the middle of each pastry square. Brush the edges of the pastry with water. Bring one corner over to meet the other and press the edges to seal. Make a small incision with your knife in the top of each turnover to allow steam to escape.

5. Arrange half of the turnovers on the baking tray. Make a glaze by mixing together the egg yolks and milk, then brush each turnover and sprinkle over the demerara sugar. Bake in the oven for about 15 minutes until golden and puffed up. Eat warm or cold.

 FREEZE:
Follow the recipe up to the end of step 4. Place on to a tray lined with baking parchment, cover and flash-freeze; once frozen solid, store in a labelled resealable freezer bag.

 FREEZER TO TABLE:
Transfer the turnovers to a baking tray lined with baking parchment and glaze as explained in step 5. Bake in an oven preheated to 200°C/180°C fan/Gas Mark 6 for 25–30 minutes until golden, puffed up and hot through.

Vanilla Cardamom Rice Pudding

SERVES 8 (4 FOR NOW AND 4 FOR LATER) • 5 MINUTES PREP • 45 MINUTES COOKING

I find utter solace in a large creamy bowlful of this, topped simply with a handful of raisins. In fact, it is the perfect canvas on which to add other flavours or ingredients, be it fruit, chocolate or nut. As the cooking time is on the longer side for a quick midweek indulgence, why wouldn't you batch-cook and freeze it, to eat hot or cold during busier times?

200g arborio risotto rice

1.2 litres milk

4 tbsp demerara sugar

6 tsp vanilla extract

10 cardamom pods, smashed

TRY ADDING:

— slices of soft mango or dried fruits

SWAP THE VANILLA AND CARDAMOM FOR:

— *nutmeg, cinnamon or even bay leaf and lemon zest*

1. Put all the ingredients into a saucepan and place over a low heat for 45 minutes, stirring often until thick and creamy.

FREEZE:
Allow to cool completely. Line the holes of a muffin tin with greaseproof paper, with some overhang. Fill the muffin holes with the rice pudding, cover with foil and put into the freezer to flash-freeze. Once frozen, remove from the tin and place in a labelled resealable freezer bag.

FREEZER TO TABLE:
Put the rice pudding portions into a small lidded saucepan and place over a low-medium heat until defrosted, then add a splash of milk and heat until warm through. Or defrost overnight in the fridge, before reheating on the hob, or warming up in the microwave in a covered bowl in short bursts, stirring between each burst, with a little extra milk so it doesn't dry out. You can also eat it cold.

Baked Berry Slump

SERVES 8 (4 FOR NOW AND 4 FOR LATER) • 10 MINUTES PREP • 45 MINUTES COOKING

Think of this slump (what a wonderful word to say!) as a baked berry base with a simple sponge cake topping, very similar to a cobbler. It is the easiest thing to make. As the fruit bubbles up under the cake batter, it does glorious things to this divine comfort pud. (Tastes great eaten cold from the fridge too, I may add!)

200g butter

100g golden caster sugar, plus 2 tbsp

4 eggs

2 tsp vanilla extract

300g self-raising flour

500g mixed fresh or frozen berries

½ tsp ground cinnamon

½ tsp ground ginger

1. Preheat the oven to 200°C/180°C fan/Gas Mark 6.

2. Beat the butter and sugar together until light and fluffy, then beat in the eggs and vanilla extract and finally fold in the flour.

3. Divide the fruit between 2 small deep ovenproof dishes, lining one with foil first, allowing some overhang. Sprinkle over the extra 2 tablespoons of sugar and the spices, give a little mix then top with the sponge mixture. Bake one in the oven for 45-50 minutes until the fruit is bubbling and hot and the sponge is cooked on top. Serve warm with vanilla ice cream or custard.

❋ *Ice Kitchen Tip*
Fresh (previously unfrozen) berries and fruit can be flash-frozen on a covered tray, then transferred to a resealable freezer bag. Or bag up into smoothie portions ready to be blitzed.

 FREEZE:
Before filling the dish, line it with foil, allowing some overhang. Fill the dish as described in step 3, then bake as above. Allow to cool completely, then cover the dish and place in the freezer to flash-freeze. Once solid, gently prise out of the deep dish and wrap well in more foil. Label and return to the freezer.

 FREEZER TO TABLE:
Unwrap and return to the baking dish, then cover with foil and bake in an oven preheated to 200°C/180°C fan/Gas Mark 6 for 35-40 minutes until piping hot through.

Proper Ice Cream Sandwiches

MAKES 8 BARS (OR 16 SMALLER SQUARES) · 20 MINUTES PREP · 10 MINUTES COOKING

This is a gem of a recipe if you're looking for pure nostalgia food. The flavour of the biscuit isn't overly sweet so it really works well with the ice cream. Make your own No Churn Ice Cream (see page 168), or do what I do when I can't even be bothered to do that (I mean, this is UTTER LAZINESS): buy it! These freezer treats are so chilled (and meant to be!). Get stocked up for summer, and all year round really. There is something quite satisfying about opening your freezer drawer and pulling out individually wrapped ice cream sandwiches, like having your own ice cream van!

100g butter

100g caster sugar

1 egg, beaten

1 tsp vanilla extract

pinch of salt

100g plain flour

3 heaped tbsp cocoa powder

2 x 500ml tubs ice cream, softened (cookies and cream, vanilla or chocolate work really well)

1. Preheat the oven to 200°C/180°C fan/Gas Mark 6 and grease and line a 30 x 22cm baking tin with baking parchment.

2. Cream the butter and sugar together until soft and fluffy, then whisk in the egg, vanilla and salt. Sift in the flour and cocoa and fold in until evenly combined.

3. Spread the batter into the lined tin and bake for about 10 minutes until just dry and starting to pull away from the edges of the tin. Leave to cool in the tin.

4. Cut the biscuit in half, lengthways. Spread the softened ice cream, as evenly as possible over one half of the biscuit. Top with the remaining half, flat side down.

FREEZE:
Wrap the whole sandwich well in foil, then put into the freezer for a few hours to firm up. Once firm, unwrap and slice into 8 bars (or 16 squares) with a sharp knife dipped in hot water, then individually double-wrap each one first in baking parchment or greaseproof paper, then tightly with foil. Label and return to the freezer.

FREEZER TO TABLE:
Defrost the ice cream sandwiches for about 5 minutes at room temperature, until the ice cream has softened a little, then eat immediately.

No Churn Ice Cream

SERVES 8–12 • 5 MINUTES PREP

Creamy ice cream without the need for a fancy machine or elbow grease has got to be one of the greatest inventions. And only three ingredients too. This is a wonderful canvas for a host of flavours, swirls and toppings. Did I mention how simple it was too? My favourite swirl is salted caramel with the addition of tamarind paste: the mixture of salt, sour, sweet is addictive. Or add some Salted Caramel Ripple Cookie Dough (see page 156).

2 x 397g tins condensed milk
600ml double cream
large pinch of sea salt
2 tsp vanilla extract

TRY ADDING (AT STEP 2):

— Swirl through peanut butter, or salted caramel with an added spoonful of tamarind for something a little more exotic

— Chopped strawberries

— Oreo cookies or cookie dough (see page 156)

1. Pour all the ingredients into a large bowl and use an electric whisk to whisk together until thick and fluffy and an indentation remains if you poke it with your finger.

2. Pour the mixture into a large freezerproof container.

 FREEZE:
Label and put into the freezer for 6 hours or so, until it reaches ice cream consistency.

 FREEZER TO TABLE:
Let the ice cream defrost at room temperature for 5–10 minutes before serving until soft enough to scoop.

Oreo Peanut Butter Ice Cake

SERVES 12–16 (6–8 FOR NOW AND 6–8 FOR LATER) • 20 MINUTES PREP • 3 HOURS FREEZING TIME

This decadent 'cake' is the simplest thing to throw together and is kind of like the love child of a cheesecake and a mousse cake. A big glug of a cream-based liqueur, like Baileys, works well in the mix too. Don't skimp on the pre-eating defrosting time though.

oil, for greasing

2 x 180g tubs cream cheese

about 200g smooth peanut butter

½ tsp sea salt flakes

300ml double cream

2 heaped tbsp (about 40g) icing sugar

1½ tbsp cocoa powder

2 tsp vanilla extract

3 x 192g boxes of Oreo thins

milk, for dunking

FOR THE TOPPING
(GO ALL OUT HERE):

— crushed Oreo cookies

— chocolate sauce

— caramel popcorn

— crushed salted peanuts

1. Oil a 20cm springform cake tin and line it with greaseproof paper.

2. In a large bowl, beat together the cream cheese and peanut butter with the salt until well combined.

3. In a separate bowl, whisk the double cream with the icing sugar, cocoa powder and vanilla extract until soft peaks remain when the whisk is removed. Gently fold this into the peanut butter mixture until well incorporated.

4. Arrange a single layer of milk-dunked Oreo cookies in the base of the cake tin: simply dunk each one in a glass of milk before you put it into the tin. When you have created a single layer, smooth over some of the peanut butter mixture. Add another layer of milk-dunked Oreo cookies, placing the layer in such a way so that it doesn't sit directly above the bottom layer. Continue the layering of peanut butter mixture with the Oreo cookies, until you have used them all up, ending with a layer of the peanut butter mixture on top. Sprinkle or spread over your choice of toppings.

 FREEZE:
Wrap the whole cake tin in foil and freeze for at least 3 hours. You can serve whole or slice into portions before putting individual foil-wrapped slices back into the freezer.

 FREEZER TO TABLE:
Before serving defrost the whole cake at room temperature for 20–30 minutes until easy to slice. Or if you have frozen individual slices, defrost for 5–10 minutes until softened.

Frozen Yoghurt Bark

SERVES 8 (4 FOR NOW AND 4 FOR LATER) • 10 MINUTES PREP

This makes a refreshing alternative to the usual iced treats on warm days but it is also quite a lovely touch at dinner parties - it will be passed around until totally devoured, I assure you. I find it therapeutic to make; there's nothing more satisfying than studding fruit and nuts into a smooth lake of thick yoghurt. Make it as decadent or as whole-some as you like - try adding toffee pieces or swirls of salted caramel.

2 x 600g tubs Greek yoghurt

6 tbsp honey

2 tsp ground cinnamon

2 tsp vanilla extract

2 large handfuls of desiccated coconut

2 large handfuls of dark chocolate chips (or roughly chop dark chocolate bar)

2 large handfuls of frozen (or fresh) berries

2 large handfuls of chopped nuts (pecans, walnuts or hazelnuts are my favourite)

SWAP THE BERRIES FOR:

— *tropical fruit, like mango and kiwi*

SWAP THE CINNAMON AND VANILLA FOR:

— *cardamom*

1. Mix everything together, except for the chocolate, berries and nuts.

2. Line a baking tray with baking parchment. Spread the yoghurt mix on to the paper, to a thickness of about 1cm. Stud with the chocolate, berries and nuts.

 FREEZE:
Cover the baking tray with foil and put into the freezer until firm, about 4-6 hours. Break into shards and store in a labelled resealable freezer bag.

 FREEZER TO TABLE:
Place the shards in the fridge to defrost and soften for just a couple of minutes before serving. (If left out of the freezer for more than 10 minutes, the bark will melt.)

Watermelon Sherbet

SERVES 6–8 • 20 MINUTES PREP

Sherbet is slap-bang in between a creamy ice cream and an icy, refreshing sorbet, with an almost bubblegum texture. It is a perfect way to show off the juiciness of watermelon; the key here is really to find a beautifully sweet specimen. The perfect antidote to sticky summer days!

4 gelatine leaves

600g ripe watermelon flesh, seeds picked out

1 tbsp lime juice

75g caster sugar

pinch of salt

100ml double cream

2 tbsp good-quality white rum

1 tsp natural red food colouring (optional)

1. Soak the gelatine leaves in cold water for 5 minutes.

2. In the meantime, blitz together the watermelon, lime juice, sugar and salt in a food processor until smooth. Pour the mixture into a bowl and set aside.

3. Squeeze out any excess water from the gelatine and add it to a small saucepan with 100ml water. Dissolve over a low heat, stirring often.

4. Add the dissolved gelatine to the watermelon mixture, along with the double cream, rum and food colouring. Stir until well combined, then put into the fridge to chill for 30 minutes, or stand the bowl in a larger bowl of iced water, until cool.

❄ *Ice Kitchen Tip*
Freeze any leftover citrus zest or juice separately in ice-cube trays, then transfer to labelled resealable freezer bags once frozen solid.

 FREEZE:
When the watermelon mixture is cool, transfer it to an ice-cream maker and freeze, following the manufacturer's instructions. Alternatively, transfer the mixture to a small freezerproof container with a lid and freeze for 1 hour, then remove from the freezer and use a fork or electric whisk to really churn through the sherbet, breaking up the ice crystals so that the mixture is all the same consistency. Return to the freezer for another 2–3 hours, whisking it about every 30 minutes, then lay a sheet of foil on the surface and freeze until it is as firm as ice cream. Don't forget to label the container.

 FREEZER TO TABLE:
Let the sherbet defrost at room temperature for 5–10 minutes until soft enough to scoop.

Mango Mojito Granita

SERVES 8–12 • 10 MINUTES PREP

A cocktail in slushie form ... what's not to love? I usually serve these up in shot glasses if it's a fancy occasion, if not, bring out the pint glass! In all seriousness though, this is a delicious way to serve a 'drink'. Of course you can leave out the rum, or try a different spirit entirely. Cachaça works beautifully too.

6 ripe mangoes, peeled, stone removed and flesh roughly chopped

zest and juice of 3 limes

24 mint leaves, roughly chopped, plus 6 small mint sprigs, to garnish

9 tbsp good-quality dark rum

caster sugar, to taste

SWAP THE MANGOES FOR:
— *berries or other fruit*

1. In a large bowl, using a hand-held blender, blitz the mangoes, lime zest and juice and the mint leaves until smooth.

2. Add the rum and give it a stir. Add the caster sugar, if needed, to taste.

❄ *Ice Kitchen Tip*
Any leftover mint can be chopped up, portioned and popped into ice-cube trays (covered) to freeze, then placed in labelled resealable freezer bags, for use in cooked dishes.

 FREEZE:
Divide the mango 'mojito' between two freezerproof containers and place in the freezer for about 7 hours, until solid.

 FREEZER TO TABLE:
About 3–5 minutes before serving, remove the granita from the freezer to defrost it a little, then use a fork to scrape it until you get a light fluffy texture all the way through. Scoop this into martini or shot glasses and garnish with a small mint leaf. Serve immediately.

Ice-cube Drinks Boosters

This is really what ice-cube trays were meant for – why freeze water when you can freeze lots of colourful, tasty and cleverly combined ingredients (and odds and ends that were destined for the bin) to revolutionise the way you serve your drinks! Once the cubes are frozen solid, pop out into resealable freezer bags for easy access.

Mary Cubes

Chop celery into pieces small enough to fit inside an ice cube and pop a piece in each hole, along with a couple of celery leaves. Generously sprinkle some sea salt and freshly cracked black pepper in each, add a few dashes of Tabasco and Worcestershire sauce (depending on how strong you like it) and top with lemon juice. For an extra kick add a little grated fresh horseradish. Add the frozen cubes to your Virgin or Bloody Marys.

Pimm's Cubes

Put small pieces of cucumber and strawberry into each ice-cube tray hole, add mint leaves and small pieces of orange and top with lemonade. Add to your Pimm's.

Water Infuser Cubes

Try adding any choice of fruit, crush it a little, pop it into an ice-cube tray, along with an intact version, e.g. some lemon juice with a slice of lemon, crushed raspberries with a whole raspberry, or crushed blueberries with a whole blueberry. Top up with water and freeze until solid. Add to your water, for a special infused twist. Or simply add mint leaves, cucumber pieces or small sprigs of rosemary to your usual water-filled ice cubes.

Fudgesicles

MAKES ABOUT 8 • 5 MINUTES PREP • 5 MINUTES COOKING

Basically a creamy, spiced cocoa-y ice-creamy kind of thing on a stick. Delicious. I tend to use silicone ice-lolly moulds that allow the ice lollies to easily pop out without having to warm the mould first.

6 tbsp cocoa powder
1 tbsp cornflour
750g milk
600ml double cream
300g chocolate chips
2 tbsp vanilla extract
1 tsp ground cinnamon
pinch of sea salt flakes

1. Make a paste with the cocoa powder, cornflour, and 4 tablespoons of the milk.

2. Put the paste into a saucepan with all the remaining ingredients and thicken over a low heat for about 5–10 minutes. Allow to cool, then pour into ice-lolly moulds.

 FREEZE:
Put the filled moulds into the freezer and freeze until the fudgesicles are solid. For a creamier lolly, stir the lollies every 30 minutes for the first 3 hours. You can then pop them out and store in a labelled resealable freezer bag.

 FREEZER TO TABLE:
Simply pop out a fudgesicle if your mould allows, otherwise, if rigid, run the mould of the fudgesicle you wish to remove under hot water until loosened enough to pull out.

Popsicles

Ice lolly, popsicle – call it what you will, this summer staple can be made by simply whizzing together your favourite fruit combo for a refreshing ready-to-go treat. Here are a few of my favourite and more unusual flavour combinations. Chop and change your popsicles by using different fruits, adding mint or citrus or sweetening with honey or icing sugar.

Coco Passion Popsicle

MAKES ABOUT 6–8 • 5 MINUTES PREP

400ml tin coconut milk
seeds and pulp of
   3 passionfruits
zest and juice of ½ lime
handful of raspberries, crushed
honey, to sweeten

1. Mix together the coconut milk, passionfruits, lime zest and juice and raspberries until combined. Sweeten to taste with honey and pour into ice-lolly moulds.

Strawberry Balsamic Popsicle

MAKES ABOUT 4–6 • 5 MINUTES PREP

500g ripe strawberries,
   hulled
5 tsp balsamic glaze
honey, to sweeten

1. Put the strawberries in a bowl with the balsamic glaze and leave to macerate for 20 minutes. Blitz the mixture in a blender and sweeten to taste with honey. Pour into ice-lolly moulds.

FREEZE:
Put the filled moulds into the freezer and freeze until the fudgesicles are solid. For a creamier lolly, stir the lollies every 30 minutes for the first 3 hours. You can then pop them out and store in a labelled resealable freezer bag.

FREEZER TO TABLE:
Simply pop out a fudgesicle if your mould allows, otherwise, if rigid, run the mould of the fudgesicle you wish to remove under hot water until loosened enough to pull out.

Instant Berry Fro-yo

SERVES 8 · 2 MINUTES PREP

This is a very clever way of using frozen berries to make a delicious treat in seconds. You need to keep a close eye on it when you are blending as it can very quickly turn into a berry yoghurt shake!

2 x 450–500g pots Greek yoghurt

enough frozen berries to fill 4 of the above empty yoghurt pots

2 frozen bananas, peeled and chopped

honey, to sweeten

TRY ADDING:

— 1 tsp ground cinnamon
— 1 tbsp finely chopped mint

1. Put all the ingredients into a blender or a food processor and pulse for a few minutes, stopping as soon as the mixture is smooth and blended to frozen yoghurt consistency – don't overmix. Eat immediately.

 FREEZE:
Transfer the fro-yo to a freezerproof container, cover with a lid, label and store in the freezer.

 FREEZER TO TABLE:
Let the fro-yo defrost at room temperature for 5 minutes until soft enough to scoop.

Iced Berries & White Chocolate Sauce

SERVES 8 (4 FOR NOW AND 4 FOR LATER) • 5 MINUTES PREP • 25 MINUTES COOKING

As well known as this simple – but ever so elegant – dessert is, it still deserves a place in a book about freezer recipes. Simple as.

800g white chocolate
600ml double cream
2 tsp vanilla extract
a couple of splashes of dark rum
½ tsp ground cinnamon
1kg frozen mixed berries

1. Place a small heatproof bowl over a saucepan of barely simmering water, making sure the bottom of the bowl doesn't touch the water. Add the white chocolate and cream to the bowl and heat gently until melted and smooth, about 25 minutes. Add the vanilla, rum and cinnamon and stir together.

2. Take the berries out of the freezer about 5 minutes before serving. Pour the hot chocolate sauce over the berries and serve immediately.

➜ **Try with** fresh mint leaves.

FREEZE:
Freeze any leftover white chocolate sauce flat in a labelled resealable freezer bag, before 'filing' upright.

FREEZER TO TABLE:
Defrost the white chocolate sauce at room temperature before gently reheating, stirring constantly, in a small heatproof bowl set over a saucepan of barely simmering water.

Appendix I
What Else to Freeze?

Personally, I find it far more useful to freeze full meals rather than freezing odds and ends of ingredients, which often spend a little time in icy limbo before inevitably ending up in the bin. But, nonetheless, here are some basic guidelines on commonplace ingredients for you.

Dairy and Eggs

	FREEZE	DEFROST
Milk	Freeze in freezerproof containers with enough room for expansion (not glass).	Defrost in the fridge overnight (shake well after defrosting).
Butter	Freeze in the original packaging, slipped into a resealable freezer bag. Slice off exactly the amount needed using a hot knife. Flavoured butters (see pages 127–129) can be frozen in ice-cube trays before being transferred to labelled resealable freezer bags.	Defrost in the fridge overnight.
Hard cheese	Grate hard cheese, then freeze in a resealable freezer bag.	Use grated cheese from frozen. If you are freezing whole blocks of cheese, note that it can become quite crumbly on defrosting.

	FREEZE	DEFROST
Yoghurt and cream	Not suitable for freezing as they can become watery and grainy, although leftover double cream can be whipped and then frozen in ice-cube trays, to be used in cooked dishes.	Defrost in the fridge overnight, or at room temperature to be used immediately.
Raw eggs	Whole beaten eggs and egg whites can be poured into ice-cube trays, covered and frozen until sold, then transferred to resealable freezer bags. Egg yolks on their own don't freeze well (they become gelatinous on defrosting) but adding a tiny pinch of salt or ¼ tsp sugar per yolk will help this. Freeze as above and don't forget to label them.	Defrost in the fridge overnight, or at room temperature to be used immediately.
Cooked eggs	Cooked egg whites (for example on a hard-boiled egg) don't freeze well as they become rubbery when defrosted. However, hard-boiled egg yolks can be frozen. Scrambled eggs freeze well: cook them so they are slightly undercooked and runny, allow to cool and then portion into muffin tins. Cover, freeze and then transfer to labelled resealable freezer bags.	Defrost hard-boiled egg yolks and scrambled eggs in the fridge overnight.

Baked Goods and Pastry

	FREEZE	DEFROST
Cooked breads and un-iced cakes	Freeze in labelled resealable freezer bags. Freezing sliced bread means you can take out exactly what you need and put straight into the toaster.	Bread can be defrosted at room temperature, then put into an oven preheated to 200°C/180°C fan/Gas Mark 6 for 5 minutes to 'refresh' the just-baked texture. Cakes should be defrosted at room temperature.
Doughs and batters	Cookie dough can be frozen in labelled foil-wrapped cylinders, then sliced into discs and baked from frozen (see page 156).	Defrost in the fridge overnight.
Breadcrumbs	Put into labelled resealable freezer bags and freeze flat.	Use straight from frozen for cooked dishes or defrost at room temperature for 30 minutes.
Pastry	This is best frozen in foil then put into a resealable freezer bag to ensure it doesn't dry out. You can loosely roll pastry sheets before double-wrapping. Make sure you do not refreeze previously frozen pastry.	Defrost in the fridge overnight, or at room temperature to be used immediately. Filo pastry is often found in the freezer section of supermarkets so will need to be defrosted before using. Make sure you keep it in its wrapping to avoid it drying out. Note that you won't be able to refreeze it in its uncooked state, so for recipes like Feta Spinach Filo Pie and Cheat's Vegetable Samosas (see pages 43 and 95), you'll need to use fresh (previously unfrozen) filo pastry if you want to freeze it.

Fruit, Veg and Herbs

	FREEZE	DEFROST
Berries and bananas	Ripe berries and bananas (peeled and sliced for convenience) can be flash-frozen until solid in a single layer on a tray before being transferred to labelled resealable freezer bags.	Fruit that has been frozen tends to turn quite mushy once defrosted so isn't ideal to eat as fresh; however, it works wonderfully in smoothies, compotes and jams (see pages 159, 162 and 35) and desserts that are to be cooked. Try using berries in their frozen state (see Iced Berries & White White Chocolate Sauce on page 181).
Other fruit	Apples, pears, plums and mangoes can be sliced, peeled (if necessary), cored or deseeded, cut up and frozen in portions in labelled resealable freezer bags, ready for blitzing to make smoothies and ice lollies, or turned into crumbles and compotes. You can also flash-freeze larger amounts in a single layer on a tray (so it doesn't freeze in one massive lump!), before being transferred to freezer bags, so you can take from the bag only what you need.	Defrost overnight in the fridge, or at room temperature if using immediately, or cook from frozen.
Citrus fruit	Lemons and limes can be frozen whole; you can freeze slices or wedges but they tend to dry out. Freeze the juice and zest separately in ice-cube trays (covered), then transfer to labelled resealable freezer bags once frozen solid. Zesting citrus when frozen is slightly easier than when fresh.	To defrost whole citrus fruit: hold under warm running water for a few seconds. Frozen citrus zest or juice ice cubes can be used from frozen in cooked dishes, or defrosted in the fridge or at room temperature.

Fruit, Veg and Herbs (continued)

	FREEZE	DEFROST
Raw vegetables	Onions and garlic can be thinly sliced or chopped and then flash-frozen in a single layer on a tray, then put into labelled freezer bags. Generally, it is best to blanch other veg in boiling water for a few minutes before freezing as this helps preserve their colour, flavour and nutrients. After blanching, plunge them into a bowl of iced water, then drain and arrange on a tray lined with kitchen paper. Flash-freeze until solid, then transfer to resealable freezer bags. I often create bags of mixed veg for my freezer; it's a convenient way to bulk up or create meals (without the faff of veg prep!) for quick midweek cooking.	You can cook veg straight from frozen.
Cooked vegetables	Flash-freeze on a covered tray, then transfer to a resealable freezer bag to pick off what you need.	Use straight from frozen.
Potatoes	Don't freeze raw potatoes! They become mushy after defrosting. However, mashed potato and roasted potatoes can be cooled, transferred to resealable freezer bags and frozen flat.	Defrost in the fridge or at room temperature, or cook from frozen.
Salads	Don't freeze! Instead make tomatoes (tinned or fresh) into tomato sauce and freeze in batches (see Swift Salvation Tomato Sauce on page 115).	Anything with a high water content, like cucumber, tomatoes and lettuce, doesn't freeze well as it becomes mushy on defrosting.

Fruit, Veg and Herbs (continued)

	FREEZE	DEFROST
Herbs	Soft herbs can be finely chopped, popped into ice-cube trays, covered and frozen. Once frozen solid, transfer to labelled resealable freezer bags. Woody herbs like thyme and rosemary can be frozen in whole sprigs in labelled freezer bags.	All can be used from frozen in cooking; soft herbs don't work as well for garnishes as they do when fresh (see page 125 for more tips on freezing herbs).

Meat

	FREEZE	DEFROST
Sausages	Remove them from their packaging and store in labelled resealable freezer bags. Sausages can be refrozen once cooked into a meal.	Defrost overnight in the fridge, or cook from frozen.
Bacon	Remove the packaging, then either freeze in portions in labelled freezer bags, or separate each slice with a little greaseproof paper before freezing in a labelled freezer bag. Bacon can be refrozen once it is cooked into a meal.	Defrost overnight in the fridge or leave out to defrost at room temperature if you plan to use it immediately.

Meat (continued)

	FREEZE	DEFROST
Small pieces of boneless chicken, pork or beef	Freeze steaks and fillets in individual portions, or cut into strips and flash-freeze on a tray before transferring to a labelled resealable freezer bag, so you can take exactly what you need and throw it straight into my quick and easy recipes with no need to defrost. Can be refrozen once it is cooked into a meal.	Defrost overnight in the fridge, or use strips straight from frozen.
Cooked chicken	Shred leftover chicken from the bone and flash-freeze on a covered tray, then transfer to a labelled, resealable freezer bag to pick off what you need.	Cooks well from frozen in soups, stews and pies.
Bone-in portions and larger joints of chicken, pork or beef	I find it best to freeze once cooked into a meal. Otherwise, remove it from its original packaging (which can take up unnecessary space and any air trapped inside can cause freezer burn) and wrap in foil, or pack into a labelled resealable freezer bag. Can be refrozen once it is cooked into a meal.	Defrost in the fridge overnight, or for up to 48 hours, depending on the size of the portion or joint. Make sure you keep the meat wrapped and place in a bowl in the bottom of the fridge to collect any defrosting liquid; this prevents any cross-contamination in the fridge. Cook as soon as possible.

Fish and Seafood

	FREEZE	DEFROST
Whole fish	Freeze as fresh as possible and make sure it hasn't previously been frozen. Gut, wash and dry, then freeze in labelled resealable freezer bags.	Defrost overnight in the fridge.
Fillets	Freeze as fresh as possible and make sure it hasn't previously been frozen. Skin if you wish and then freeze in labelled resealable freezer bags. Small fillets can be cooked from frozen.	Defrost overnight in the fridge.
Seafood	Freeze as fresh as possible and make sure it hasn't previously been frozen. Seafood (like squid and small shellfish) can be frozen raw (as long as it is previously unfrozen) or cooked, cooled and immediately frozen. It is best to flash-freeze seafood on a covered tray, then transfer to a labelled resealable freezer bag (so it doesn't freeze in one large lump). Seafood can be used from frozen.	Defrost overnight in the fridge, or cook straight from frozen.

Rice and Pasta

	FREEZE	DEFROST
Rice	Freeze any excess cooked rice as soon as possible after it cools (rice left out at room temperature for too long has a greater risk of developing harmful bacteria or toxins). Bag up in individual portions in resealable freezer bags.	Defrost overnight in the fridge. Individual portions can be cooked from frozen either on the hob or in the microwave. With both methods you need to stir often to ensure that the rice is piping hot through.
Pasta	Fresh uncooked pasta can be tossed in flour to keep strands separate, then flash-frozen on a covered tray and stored in portions in a resealable freezer bag. I wouldn't recommend freezing cooked pasta as the texture will change on defrosting; however, it can be frozen as part of a complete meal, such as the Minestrone on page 71 or a pasta bake.	Cook from frozen (add straight into boiling water).

Wine and Stock

	FREEZE	DEFROST
Wine	Freeze in ice-cube trays.	Frozen wine ice cubes can be used from frozen in cooked dishes.
Stock	Freeze in labelled, resealable freezer bags in portions. Or reduce to make a thick concentrated stock and freeze in ice-cube trays.	Cook from frozen (add straight to boiling water).

Appendix II
Vegetarian and Vegan Recipes (and Swaps)

So many of the Ice Kitchen recipes are vegetarian, or can become vegetarian (or vegan) with a quick chop and change of a few ingredients. Please find below a list of those recipes, with the vegan versions (where applicable), bracketed. Don't let this stop you making your own veggie versions of some of the other recipes in this book though!

Breakfast & Brunch
Zap-n-Go Morning Muffins (Vegan: swap the dairy for vegan alternatives; swap honey for agave syrup)
Sweetcorn Fritters
Cinna-berry Pancakes
Ice Kitchen Oats (Vegan: use non-dairy milk)
Cheddar French Toast
Fridge Forage Frittatas
Brown Sugar Banana Bread
Ice Kitchen Jam
Breakfast Beans (Use veggie sausages and leave out the bacon)

Main Meals
QUICK (30 minutes or less)
Creole Gumbo (Vegan: swap the chicken, sausage and prawns for sweet potato and sweetcorn; use vegetable stock)
Feta Spinach Filo Pie (Vegan: use vegan feta)
Lentil Chilli Non Carne (Vegan)
Coconut Prawn Curry (Vegan: swap the prawns for sweet potato or cauliflower and cook until tender)
Pineapple Fried Coconut Rice (Vegan)
Eastern Stuffed Peppers (Vegan: swap the halloumi for vegan alternative)
Jerked Mac 'N' Cheese (Vegan: swap the dairy for vegan alternatives)

Gazpacho (Vegan)
Quick Savoury Puff Tarts (Vegan: swap egg wash for non-dairy milk)

MEDIUM (45 minutes or less)
Peanut Stew (Vegan)
Indian Spiced Beans (Vegan: swap the dairy for vegan alternative)
Ginger & Turmeric Dal (Vegan: swap the dairy for vegan alternative)
Pineapple Chicken Enchiladas (Vegan: swap the chicken for vegetables)
Butternut Squash & Sage Pasta Bake (Vegan: swap the dairy for vegan alternatives)
Vegetable Toad in the Hole with Onion Gravy
Freezer Pizza (Vegan)
Carrot & Coriander Soup (Vegan)
Minestrone (Vegan)

LONGER (45 minutes plus)
Ratatouille (Vegan)
Katsu Curry (Vegan: use crumbed aubergine and vegetable stock; swap the honey for agave syrup)

Salvation Suppers
One Base Many Ways – Mixed Veg
One Base Many Ways – Mince

Swift Salvation Sauces
Tomato Sauce (Vegan)
Coconut Curry Sauce (Vegan)
Everything Sauce (Vegan: use vegetable
    stock)

Salvation Suppers: Ice Cube Sauces &
Butters
Ice Cube Honey Mustard (Vegan: swap
    the honey for agave syrup)
Pesto Mathematics (Vegan: swap the
    dairy for vegan alternative)
Ice Cube Chimmichurri (Vegan)
Buffalo Ice Cube Butter
Tomato Basil Ice Cube Butter
Blue Cheese Ice Cube Butter
Sriracha Lime Coriander Ice Cube Butter
Cinna-berry Ice Cube Butter

Snacks & Sharers
QUICK (30 minutes or less)
Falafel (Vegan)
Spiced Flatbreads (Vegan: swap the dairy
    for vegan alternatives)
Cookies & Cream Smoothie (Vegan: use
    non-dairy milk)

MEDIUM (45 minutes or less)
Jalapeño Corn Humitas
Polenta Chips (Vegan: swap the dairy for
    vegan alternative)
Cornbread
Bacon Cheese Straws (leave out the bacon)

LONGER (45 minutes plus)
Korean Cauliflower Poppers (Vegan: swap
    the dairy for vegan alternatives)
Loaded Potato Skins (leave out the
    bacon)
Thai Crab Cakes (swap the crab for peas)

Crispy Aubergine with Honey–Tamarind
    Drizzle

Puds & Cool Treats
PUDS
Salted Caramel Ripple Cookie Dough
    (Vegan: swap the dairy and salted
    caramel for vegan alternatives, or leave
    out the salted caramel)
The Simplest Cookie
Berry Compote (Vegan)
Peach Puff Tart (Vegan: swap honey for
    agave syrup and egg wash for non-dairy
    milk)
Blueberry Turnovers
Vanilla Cardamom Rice Pudding (Vegan:
    use non-dairy milk)
Baked Berry Slump

COOL TREATS
Proper Ice Cream Sandwiches
No Churn Ice Cream
Oreo Peanut Butter Ice Cake
Frozen Yoghurt Bark (Vegan: swap the
    dairy for vegan alternative; swap the
    honey for agave syrup)
Watermelon Sherbet (Vegan: swap
    the dairy for vegan alternative; use
    vegetarian gelatine)
Mango Mojito Granita (Vegan)
Fudgesicles (Vegan: swap the dairy for
    vegan alternatives)
Coco Passion Popsicle (Vegan)
Strawberry Balsamic Popsicle (Vegan)
Instant Berry Fro-Yo (Vegan: swap the
    dairy for vegan alternative)
Iced Berries & White Chocolate Sauce
    (Vegan: swap the dairy for vegan
    alternative)

Appendix III

Clever Prep Dishes

Sometimes it makes sense to make a few dishes at the same time, especially when there are crossover ingredients; chopping a few more carrots, for example, to make another meal makes much more sense than having to do it on two separate occasions. I've listed some of my favourite group-together recipes to help you plan cleverly – and avoid food waste!

BEEF (OR PORK, OR A MIX OF BOTH) MINCE
Meatloaf (page 81)
Cheat's Jamaican Beef Patties (page 84)
Salvation Suppers: One Base Many Ways: Mince Base (page 98)
Salvation Suppers: Feasts-in-Foil – Mexican Beef (page 110)

STEWING STEAK
Beef & Prune Tagine (page 76)
Beef Rendang (page 77)

SAUSAGES
Breakfast Beans (page 37)
Sausage & Lentil Hotpot (page 48)
The Simplest Sausage Rolls (page 142)

PEPPERS AND ONIONS
Creole Gumbo (page 40)
Sausage & Lentil Hotpot (page 48)
Peanut Stew (page 57)
Ratatouille (page 83)

WHITE SAUCE
Curried Fish Pie (page 49)
Jerked Mac 'N' Cheese (page 52)
Korean Cauliflower Poppers (page 148)

CARROTS AND ONIONS
Lentil Chilli Non-Carne (page 44)
Carrot & Coriander Soup (page 70)
Minestrone (page 71)
Katsu Curry Sauce (page 86)
Salvation Suppers: One Base Many Ways: Mince Base (page 98)
Swift Salvation Everything Sauce (page 117)

SWEETCORN AND SPRING ONIONS:
Sweetcorn Fritters (page 25)
Jalapeño Corn Humitas (page 138)
Cornbread (page 141)

TOMATOES (TINNED AND FRESH)
Gazpacho (page 53)
Minestrone (page 71)
Ratatouille (page 83)
Swift Salvation Tomato Sauce (page 115)

COCONUT MILK
Beef Rendang (page 77)
Swift Salvation Coconut Curry Sauce (page 116)
Pineapple Fried Coconut Rice (page 46)
Coconut Prawn Curry (page 45)
Coco Passion Popsicles (page 177)

Appendix IV

Feasting Menu Ideas

CAJUN HEAT

Sweet Potato & Chorizo Hash (page 36)
Creole Gumbo – leave out the chorizo so you don't double up (page 40)
Cornbread (page 141)
Winger Winger Chicken Wings Dinner with Buffalo Butter (pages 151 and 127)

Serve with plain rice and fresh leafy salads and finish with Blueberry Turnovers and ice cream (page 162)

BBQ FEAST

Jerked Mac 'N' Cheese (page 52)
Sticky Ribs with Chimmichurri (pages 82 and 124)
Jalapeño Corn Humitas (page 138)
Loaded Potato Skins – try a sweet potato version (page 145)

Serve with fresh salads and finish with Proper Ice Cream Sandwiches (page 167)

PARTY BITES

Pineapple Fried Coconut Rice – serve on canapé spoons (page 46)
Mini Cheat's Jamaican Beef Patties (page 84)
The Simplest Sausage Rolls – try a mix of fillings (page 142)
Bacon Cheese Straws (page 143)
Korean Cauliflower Poppers (page 148)

Finish with Iced Berries & White Chocolate Sauce (page 181) and Mango Mojito Granita (page 173)

EASTERN SPICE

Eastern Stuffed Peppers (page 50)
Falafel (page 132)
Spiced Flatbreads (page 135)
Lamb, Cherry & Pine Nut Meatballs (page 136)
Crispy Aubergine with Honey-Tamarind Drizzle (page 152)

Finish with Vanilla Cardamom Rice Pudding (page 163)

TEX MEX TASTES

Lentil Chilli Non-Carne (page 44)
Pineapple Chicken Enchiladas (page 60)
Chipotle Pulled Pork (page 78)

Serve with coriander rice, guacamole, salsa, tortilla chips and soft or crunchy tacos and finish with Watermelon Sherbet (page 172)

ASIAN FRESH

Beef Rendang (page 77)
Thai Crab Cakes (page 144)
Ice Cube Nuoc Cham (page 120) over cold rice noodles, with coriander, grated carrot and peas

Serve with turmeric spiced rice and finish with Coco Passion Popsicles (page 177)

INDIAN WARMERS

Coconut Prawn Curry (page 45)
Indian Spiced Beans (page 58)
Ginger & Turmeric Dal (page 59)
Spiced Flatbreads (page 135)

Serve with pilau rice and finish with Frozen Yoghurt Bark – add ½ teaspoon ground green cardamom (page 170)

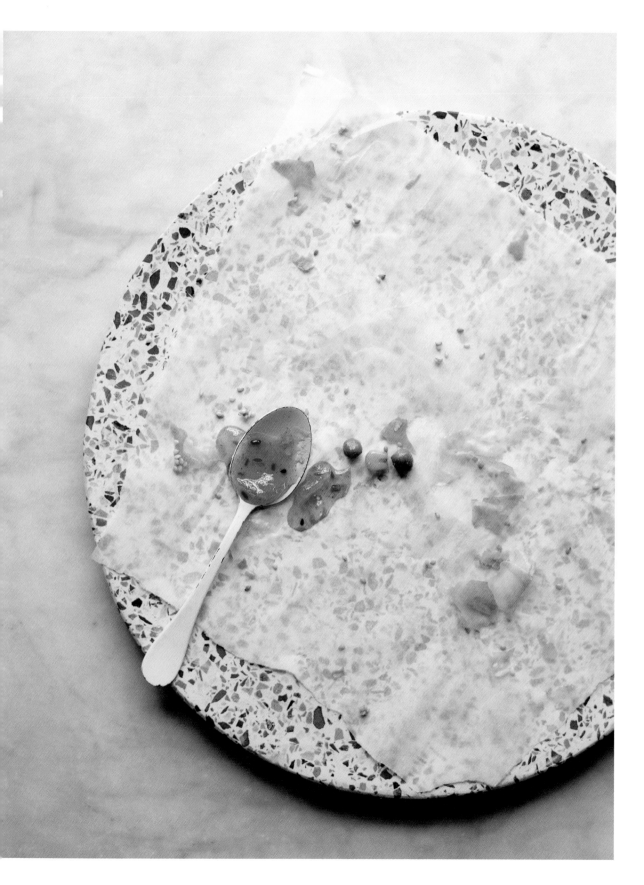

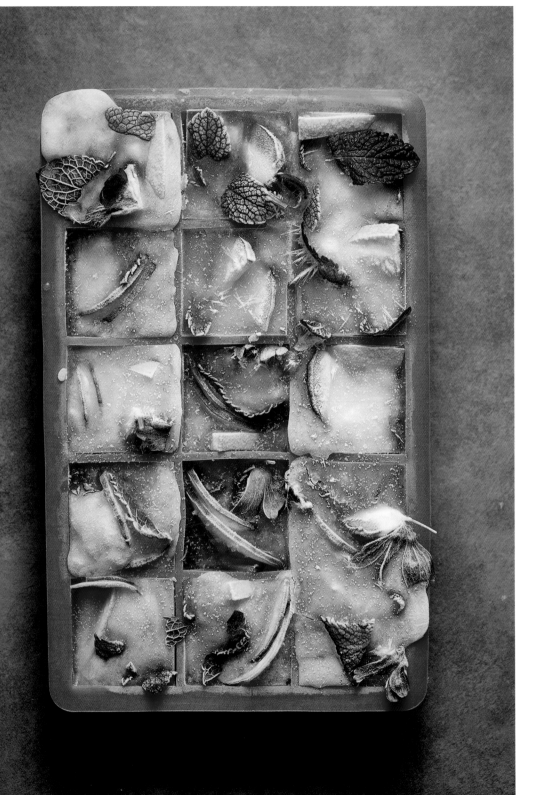

Index

Acknowledgements

The most sincere thanks to the stellar and truly lovely team behind this book: Katya, Sarah and James. Katya, your enthusiasm and excitement for this project has been so, so motivating. To Andrew, Emily, Flossy, Carole, Lisa and Olivia: thank you for the perfectly delicious images and mega-fun photography days – dare I say they felt like mini-holidays to me? I miss the random chat and shoot food loot (although my waistline doesn't!).

Thanks as always to my fabulous agent, Antony, for all your feedback, support and suggestions.

To my lovely friends and family, who tried out recipes, answered my questions about their freezer habits, brought me cups of tea to warm up my frozen fingers and supported me over these last few months. I hope you love the book – thank you so, so much!

To Ma, for helping us out over a most hectic summer with a toddler, a newborn and a pile of recipes to test – I'm not sure how I would have done it without you and your sage advice. Your room is here waiting and we are always ready to feed you! And to you and Pa for bringing us up to appreciate food, not to waste it, and to make something tasty out of what's already there. These recipes are a testament to you.

To my little Poppy: thanks for being my writing buddy and always being close by for much-needed snuggles and/or scraps from my plate.

And to the absolute sweetest reasons I keep my freezer so well-stocked: my darling boys, Ben, Milesy and Ot ot. Thank you for inspiring all these recipes. (Even though half our miniscule freezer was taken up with breastmilk for you, Ot ot, we still made it work!)

About the Author

Shivi was born in Trinidad and loves to twist classic Caribbean dishes and ingredients from her childhood into her own vibrant, fresh and easy-to-make recipes. Her first book was *Caribbean Modern: Recipes From The Rum Islands*, and her recipes have been featured in numerous publications, including the *Sunday Times*, *Delicious* magazine, the *Metro* and the *Guardian*, to name a few. She is a regular guest on *Saturday Kitchen* and has also been featured on BBC *Woman's Hour*. She lives in London with her two small children, husband and Yorkshire terrier.

HarperCollins*Publishers*
1 London Bridge Street
London SE1 9GF

www.harpercollins.co.uk

First published by HarperCollins*Publishers* 2020

10 9 8 7 6 5 4 3 2

Text © Shivi Ramoutar 2020
Photography © Andrew Burton 2020

Shivi Ramoutar asserts the moral right to be identified as the author of this work

A catalogue record of this book is available from the British Library

ISBN 978-0-00-838511-8

Food Styling: Emily Jonzen
Prop Styling: Olivia Wardle
Design and Art Direction: James Empringham

Printed and bound by GPS Group

All rights reserved. No part of this publication may be reproduced, stored in a retrieval system, or transmitted, in any form or by any means, electronic, mechanical, photocopying, recording or otherwise, without the prior written permission of the publishers.

MIX
Paper from
responsible sources
FSC™ C007454

This book is produced from independently certified FSC™ paper to ensure responsible forest management.

For more information visit: www.harpercollins.co.uk/green